HELLO THERE!

Here's our 13th Blue Peter Book—but we're not superstitious! For us, thirteen is definitely a lucky number, because it means there's another addition to our collection of Blue Peter publications And since our Twelfth Book, we've also been able to print some of the very best of your Odd Odes which we've put in a paperback, so watch out for that, too.

We've had a year of changes—all of them good, except one very sad piece of news. Poor old Jason died of kidney failure on 16 January, aged 11 years 8 months, and even though all pet owners know that sooner or later their pets will die, it's always a blow when it happens. To us, Jason was the best cat in the world, and we know he was very much loved by all Blue Peter viewers.

Although we didn't feel we could replace Jason immediately, on 19 February we introduced our new twins. Jack and Jill are silver spotted tabbies, and if you look at their picture on page 12, you'll see how impossible it was to choose between them, so we had them both! Another new member of the team is Rags, our trainee pony for handicapped riders. You can read all about her on page 30, and see the magnificent results of our Clothes-Horse Race Appeal. Thanks to your fantastic collection of old wool and cotton, many more disabled children and adults will be able to join riding centres,

DO YOU RECOGNISE ANY OF THESE PHOTOGRAPH

4

because we've been able to give help to over 300 groups for handicapped riders all over Britain.

One of the highlights of our year has been our special link with the successful British Everest Expedition. Chris Bonington, the leader, took some Blue Peter flags to fly on the Expedition's tents. He sent us a series of exciting reports, and as soon as the Expedition returned to Britain, Chris came to the studio together with Doug Scott and Sherpa Petember who made the first successful ascent of the South-West face. Tragically, one of our friends died—film cameraman Mick Burke. We feel proud that before he joined the Expedition, Mick helped to make several of our Blue Peter films, including Peter's climb up Black Crag.

We're still doing our best to think of as many ways as possible to save money. There are two really economical recipes on page 62, including a concentrated fruitade that works out at less than 1p per glass! There are ideas for a very attractive Christmas decoration, accessories for a soldier doll, and a great idea for belts.

Turkey and Friesland, the Lake District and Cornwall are just a few places our travels have taken us. John's taken part in 6 national sporting events in *Go with Noakes*, and the new series of *Special Assignments* has featured stories about famous people and the houses they lived in. The houses are all in Britain and they're well worth a visit. There's a reminder of where they are on page 76.

We all hope you'll enjoy our 13th Book—most of the ideas in it have come from Blue Peter viewers—so it's well and truly yours!

John Noakes

Lesley Judd

Peter Purves

Jack and Jill

Petra

Shep

EY'VE ALL BEEN IN BLUE PETER. TURN TO PAGE 76 FOR THE ANSWERS.

the GENERATION GAME

Would *you* stand up in front of 20 million viewers and make a fool of yourself? That's what Generation Game contestants have been doing for the past five years, and there's a queue of hundreds of hopeful "victims" waiting to take part!

Bruce was having a quick cup of tea when we arrived at the BBC Television Theatre at Shepherd's Bush Green. In the old days before it was a studio, the theatre used to be a well-known Music Hall—the Shepherd's Bush Empire—so there's a proper stage, a place for the orchestra, and rows of seats in the stalls, circle and dress circle. For the recording of the actual show there's a real, live audience, but for the rehearsals, the theatre was full of an army of cameramen, make-up and wardrobe staff, teams of scene men to move the tables and chairs, bring all the games on and off, and put the prizes on the conveyor belt, also sound and lighting engineers—to say nothing of the production team led by Jim Moir.

Bruce explained that we were to be "stand in"

Presenting all the fun and games and slapstick is a mammoth operation for the engineers and technicians who work behind the scenes—as John and I discovered when we spent a day with Bruce Forsyth.

contestants for the rehearsal so that the games would be a complete surprise for the *real* contestants when the show was recorded in the evening.

We had to be mother and son—and that was a laugh for a start, especially when Bruce congratulated me on looking so young considering my "son" was such a well-developed lad. Even though it was only a rehearsal, Bruce and all of us "stand-in" contestants had to go through everything—just as though it was all real so that the camera crew, the director and the whole team of technicians could get a rough idea of what was going to happen—even down to Bruce's jokes and Anthea Redfern's famous twirl.

Bruce and Anthea not only have to remember

Anthea gives details of all the contestants to Bruce who reads them out. John and I had to be mother and son, which caused a lot of laughter.

Behind the scenes, Ken in charge of the Lighting Control Room, had to balance the picture quality from four different cameras.

In our second game we had precisely ninety seconds to cover five cakes with a gooey, sticky fondant. It wasn't surprising John lost one of his cakes in the bowl.

the rules for all the games, they have to make sure the contestants stand in the right positions and move on and off in the right directions. Sitting at home and watching it on the telly, you'd never realise all that goes on behind-the-scenes to make the Generation Game the slick, polished show that it is.

All the time we were answering Bruce's questions and trying out the games, the orchestra was rehearsing, the sound supervisor was checking his microphones and all his tape machines, and the powerful television lights were constantly being adjusted.

Up in the Control Room the Director, Alan, was explaining to the cameramen exactly what sort of pictures he wanted—close-ups of faces and hands and feet, full-length shots of the contestants with Bruce and Anthea, and quick reaction shots whenever anything unexpected happened—which was nearly all the time!

Altogether there were four cameras taking the different pictures and 18 microphones. One of the many problems for the director and the engineers to overcome is avoiding huge shadows of the cameras and the microphone booms being cast all over the contestants' faces, so throughout the rehearsals we had to stop and start and repeat the bits that were especially tricky for the technicians, over and over again.

Our first game was comparatively simple—a "famous couples" contest—although it's surprising how nervous you can feel when you only have a few seconds to make up your mind about the answers. The second was more like a cook's nightmare than a game. We had precisely 90 seconds to cover five cakes with a gooey, sticky fondant—and it was *very* messy. When John managed to lose one of his cakes in the bowl of fondant mixture, Bruce was quite sarcastic!

But in spite of all our mistakes, we got through to the finals, and for the last game we tossed up with the other finalists to see who would try it out first. As we lost the toss and the other couple chose to play first, we had to go into "Bruce's Room," so that we couldn't see what the other contestants were doing and gain an unfair advantage.

It's more like a box than a room—hidden right behind the scenery so that there's no view of the stage. And we had to put headphones on over which very loud music was played, so we

couldn't hear the game, either.

The game was an acting sketch where we all had to dress up. The two contestants were a French maid and a Field-Marshal in a comedy spy thriller—and the other parts were played by Bruce and the actress Liz Fraser.

So that we could speak the right words, pieces of paper with lines from the play on them were stuck all over the place. When it came to our

turn, two of mine were on the back of John's coat, and one of his was on a lampshade. It was all quite hilarious, and Shep, who was sitting watching us in the stalls, was longing to join in—especially at the end when we all died and flopped flat on the floor on a tiger skin rug.

Much to our surprise the judges decided that *we'd* won, so our next battle was answering Bruce's three general knowledge questions—to see which of us would go on to the conveyor belt.

With the score at one all, the atmosphere was tense—then the final question came: "Britain has a new World Welterweight Boxing Champion. What is his name?" Quick as a flash, John replied, "John Stracey" a fraction of a second before me.

But the surprises weren't over. John had to dash round the back of the stage to the conveyor belt and see how many objects he could remember in 45 seconds.

In the finale of the Generation Game, we played the parts of Fifi, the French maid, and a Field-Marshal. Liz Frazer and Bruce played the other parts.

John's disguise was a standard lamp.

We all enjoyed the sketch and were delighted when the judges decided that we had won.

Watching at home, this part of the programme looks perfectly calm and simple—but behind the scenes, out of sight of the viewers, it takes four men to put everything on the moving belt, and three more to take them off. All that frenzied activity, well within earshot, makes remembering what you've seen extremely hard—and I thought John did very well indeed to get 12 out of the 18 prizes—with a bit of help from Bruce! Not that he took them home, of course! They all had to go back on the belt ready for the real contestants in the evening. Still, it was all great fun and we enjoyed ourselves enormously.

By the time the rehearsal was over, we were exhausted. But Bruce and Anthea looked as fresh as a couple of daisies—and *they* had to get ready to do it all over again.

"Thanks a lot, John and Lesley," yelled Bruce as we put on our coats, and then he paid us a great compliment, turning to Anthea and the camera crew he added:

"Didn't they do well?"

And strangely enough, we felt he really meant it, too!

"IS MR JOHN NOES OF HALIFAX ERE?"

"Younger—Charlie Younger?"
Billy Kirby, the Bellman of the 1975
Grasmere Sports, looked down at his list
of contenders for the lightweight
Cumberland wrestling event.

"Is it Noakes you're after?" I asked,
wildly hoping that the mythical "Noes"
would miraculously appear in the nick of
time.

Billy held his list at arm's length and
looked again. "That's right, lad. John
Noakes of Halifax to wrestle with
Charlie Younger of Throckton."

It was the 123rd meeting of the Grasmere Sports,
where men of the Lake District meet every year to find
the champions of the Lakeland Games. The event takes
place in the Grasmere Valley surrounded by rolling
green hills, mountainous crags and shimmering lakes.
The contenders are nearly all local men, mostly
farmers (I was one of the few foreigners) and the
games are like nothing else in the world. The
wrestling is Cumberland and Westmorland style, with
strange terms like Cross Buttock, Inside Hyde and Dog
Fall. The "Guides" race is up to the top of Butter Crag,
290 metres high, and back down to the valley again. And
perhaps the most bizarre of all—the Hound Trail, with a
huge pack of hounds following an aniseed trail 10
miles through the fells. This wasn't only going to be my
first attempt at Cumberland wrestling, but my first
full-length film in the "Go With Noakes" series, so I
hoped I was going to make good.

I shook hands with Charlie Younger, and bent down
to "tak odd" which looks as though we were going to
perform a weird dance with our bottoms stuck out. The
idea is to knock your partner off his balance by
employing such ruses as "outside stroke", "back heel",
and "full buttock"—or one of the peculiar names I
mentioned earlier. The first man to touch the floor with
anything else but his feet is the loser.

And it's not just the names that are odd. The
wrestling outfit with fully embroidered, sleeveless vest,

Before the games began, I started training with ex-champion John Dennison.

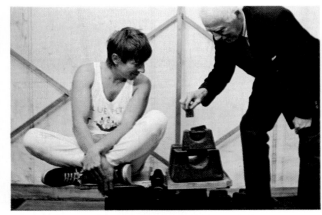

The weigh in. To qualify as a lightweight you had to weigh below eleven stone.

The real thing. Charlie Younger got me in a cross buttock and I was swung clean off my feet—

while on the other side of the field they were getting ready for the start of the hound trail.

long drawers and velvet trunks, is not what you would call *ordinary*. At the end of the day they have a prize for the most outstanding costume. I didn't win *that*, either!

I'd had a bit of training before the event with John Dennison, a local farmer who's reckoned to be one of the top light-weight wrestlers. I was frantically trying to remember some of the things he'd told me, but Charlie Younger of Throckton soon had my measure and it wasn't long before no part of me whatsoever was touching the floor! Charlie had got me in a cross buttock and I was swung off my feet! I'd hoped at least I'd get a few laughs—but the judges were not amused. Charlie Younger was the winner and I slunk off to watch the Hound Trail.

The dogs are trained to follow a scent of aniseed and paraffin which had been laid that morning by one of the organisers, Lance Footit. He drags an old rag soaked in the mixture for 10 miles over the fells, timing it so that he gets back to Grasmere just as the hounds are ready for off.

The hound trail is a very serious event at Grasmere and the betting runs high. Every owner has his own theory about the diet to feed his dog in the days running up to the race, and nobody gives away any secrets! There is a story that at one race a gang, who had all bet on one particular dog, laid a false trail through a barn with a door at either end. When the pack rushed in, they closed both doors, imprisoning all the hounds; then they released the one they wanted to win, and

when they thought he'd got a good enough start, let the rest follow. But they reckoned without the hound's pack instinct. The dog bounded along for a mile or two and then felt a bit lonely, so he sat down and waited for the rest to catch up!

Once the hounds have been released at the start, they disappear from view as they race at speeds of up to 30 mph across the fells. The owners watch their progress through binoculars, but everyone else goes to watch the other events until someone cries "Trail" as the first dogs appear over the hill. The owners by now are strung out across the finishing line yelling and waving to their dogs—and brandishing bowls full of food to encourage them over the last few yards. It's absolute pandemonium with owners bawling and hounds baying, and a brass band blaring out "John Peel" to welcome them home.

The race to the top of Butter Crag is called the "Guides Race" because it used to be run by locals who took tourists for guided walks across the fells. The track has a one in two gradient in places, and it must be one of the most gruelling races ever invented. Fred Reeves, last year's winner and much fancied for 1975, took me out on a practice run to show me the route.

"The great secret, John," he said, "apart from bein' fit, is to know the track like the back o' your hand." His great rival was Tommy Sedgewick who was not so good as Fred on the climb, but could make

The bookmakers were busy taking bets for all the races, but the odds were highest for the hound trail.

The hounds are about to be released for a ten-mile race following an aniseed trail through the fells.

The most gruelling race of them all is the "Guides Race" to the top of Butter Crag and back.

Fred Reeves was the winner.

faster speeds on the dangerous descent.

"The turn at the summit's the worst bit John. Your knees feel like water, I tell you."

For some reason I'll never understand my name was down for the heavyweight wrestling event. However, it was due to take place at the same time as the Guides Race, and while I wasn't exactly looking forward to running up Butter Crag, it seemed infinitely preferable to being crushed to death by 21-stone Wilf Brocklebank—"Big Wilf" to his fans. So I had a word with Billy Kirby, the Bellman.

"All right, I'll 'blar ye oot'," he said.

Before I could find out what that meant, he stuck up his hand in front of the crowd and said:

"John Noakes—Blue Peter and Halifax—the forst time. John Noakes—Blue Peter and Halifax—the second time. John Noakes—Blue Peter and Halifax—Blarn oot."

I never did quite understand what that was about, but it meant I didn't have to fight Big Wilf, so I gratefully went off to get ready for the Guides Race.

I discovered the record time stood at an incredible 12 minutes 57 seconds—that's nearly 10 minutes up and 3 minutes down. At the top you're given a tally which proves you've actually been there and not taken a short cut.

I was close to Fred just before the start and I asked him how he felt. He looked out of the corner of his eye at Tommy Sedgewick and confessed he was a wee bit

nervous. You are worried about winning the race, I thought, looking up at the crag. I'll be surprised if I survive!

At the first wall, Fred was well in the lead, Steve Parsons was second, and Tommy Sedgewick close behind at third. I was a little bit farther down the hill, sharing 18th place with Reg Harrison.

By the wall I was on my own. In fact, so far as I was concerned, the running bit was over until I reached the summit. My legs had already turned to jelly.

At 9 minutes 21 seconds, Fred was picking up his tally at the summit, 50 yards ahead of the field. Tommy Sedgewick was still in third place, but for Fred the worst had still to come.

I was the last to reach the top, and by the time I started on the downhill run, the race was well and truly over. Fred Reeves had done it again. The band struck up "See the Conquering Hero Comes" and the crowd roared. His time was an amazing 12 minutes 50.7 seconds—7 seconds inside his own record. Tommy Sedgewick was an easy second.

Some little time later, the band kindly and a little ironically played "See the Conquering Hero" once again, as a triumphant Noakes crossed the finishing line. But I was not alone. A dog who had lost his way in the hound trail trotted in beside me.

I had made the slowest time ever recorded in 107 years!

JACK AND JILL

Our new pets are our first ever twins. They were born on 29 January 1976, and like Jason, made their first visit to the studio when they were only three weeks old. Jack, who is on the right, has magnificent striped markings, and Jill's spots are becoming more clearly defined as she grows older.

We knew we'd be in for double trouble with twins, but although they get up to a great deal of mischief, we've never regretted our decision to keep them both.

They've learned to get on with Petra and Shep, and so far Jill seems to be the more adventurous one—but Jack once came face to face with a six-metre high inflatable Tyrannosaurus Rex and didn't even turn a whisker!

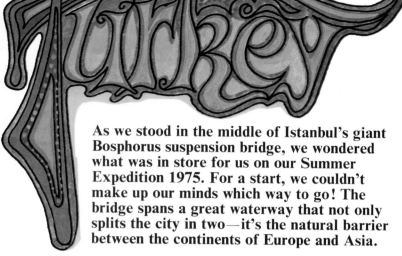

Turkey

As we stood in the middle of Istanbul's giant Bosphorus suspension bridge, we wondered what was in store for us on our Summer Expedition 1975. For a start, we couldn't make up our minds which way to go! The bridge spans a great waterway that not only splits the city in two—it's the natural barrier between the continents of Europe and Asia.

Having a bath Turkish style. In this hot room, sweat poured out by the pint!

The soapy massage nearly finished me off— but at the end I was spotless!

Gladiators once fought at Ephesus. Exploring the ancient city we found temples, theatres and a 60-seater lavatory.

"Let's start in Europe," said John. "And what's more, let's have a cup of coffee before we do anything else," added Lesley.

Turks seem to drink coffee non-stop, and it's nothing like the big, milky cups we're used to in this country. For a start it's served from a special brass pot and poured into little tiny cups that look as though they've come from a dolls tea set. There's a saying that Turkish coffee should be "black as night, sweet as love and hot as hell". It was, too; but not as hot as the Turkish bath that John and Pete went to. For a start, they lay on marble slabs in a room so hot that the sweat poured off them by the pint. Then the massage began. Thump! Wallop! Both of them were banged and pommelled to gasping point by a couple of huge men with very strong hands.

"If he does it again," groaned John, "I think I'll hit him back. But I suppose it's doing me good."

Next came the soap. Basins full of foamy lather were slopped all over them.

"I feel like a cake decoration," said Pete as he sat there looking like a snowman. Soon he was just as cold! Buckets of icy water get flung at you to finish off a Turkish bath, and by the time John and Pete left, they felt marvellous as they stepped out into the burning heat of the Istanbul streets.

As well as Turkish baths, we came across Roman ones—hot mineral springs that poured down a mountain, turning into a series of natural swimming pools. Before the Sultans came, both the Greeks and the Romans ruled Turkey and the remains of their ancient cities are still standing. Perhaps the most spectacular is Ephesus, and to walk through its streets is a great experience. We walked up marble streets lined with splendid columns, passed temples, libraries and even a 60-seater public lavatory and arrived at an immense open-air theatre, big enough to seat over 24 thousand people. The back row is so far away from the stage that from there an actor looked about the size of a toy soldier. Yet when Pete sat there and John spoke from the stage, every word sounded clear as a bell—and he didn't even have to raise his voice!

The "cotton castles" of Pamukkale are made of rock. Mineral water falls have turned them into pools.

You can swim in a cotton castle if you don't mind getting into hot water!
Guess what we found inside this mountain! A secret church and an old painting of St George of England.

St Paul came to Ephesus and he caused a riot! In his day the great goddess Diana was worshipped there, and her temple was known as one of the wonders of the Ancient world. When Paul came to teach the Christian faith, all the souvenir dealers called a great protest meeting in the theatre. They reckoned if people turned away from Diana and took to the new faith, the tourists wouldn't come to the temple and they'd lose their business. The meeting turned into a screaming mob. The Town Clerk had to come and calm the people down—and St Paul and his followers were hounded out of the city. In the end, Christianity did come to Ephesus, and when we went to see the Wonder of the Ancient World, all that was left was one column of Diana's magnificent temple, standing all by itself, in a pile of rubble. You can still get souvenirs though, and Lesley bought one.

"A bit of a come down," she said, looking at the little plastic figure of the goddess Diana, "ending up as a key tag when you used to be a Wonder of the World!"

The early Christians in Turkey struggled against terrible persecutions. When the Greeks and Romans left and the Moslems swept over Turkey they had to go into hiding. In one place, Kaymakli, they literally dug themselves in. From the surface there's nothing to be seen, yet hollowed out beneath the fields were a series of huge caves with homes, granaries, wine presses and even stables. It was a whole underground city where 100,000 people and their animals would hide for months on end, walling themselves in with huge stone doors. When we explored the city, we found one cave still in use. As we felt our way along the dark tunnels, we turned a corner and came across what must surely be the world's deepest disco! Down in the darkness, it was deafening, and on the surface faint noises coming through the air vents gave away the secret city. But when the disco's closed and there are no clues to guide you, Kaymakli's disguise is as good as ever it was.

Another place where the Christians went to hide was a valley in Cappadocia. They fortified the entrance and then started to hollow out the rock.

Turks are proud of their national costumes. They are family heirlooms and the silver jewels can be worth a fortune.

Mustapha deafened us with his hand-made drum.

In time they built churches, a monastery and a nunnery, and this strange valley became the centre of the Christian teaching. In some places, the stone had fallen away to reveal beautifully decorated churches, but mostly we had to scramble up the rock and duck in to the little doorways to see the treasures. In one we came across a surprise! There on the wall was a painting of our patron saint, St George. We'd completely forgotten that St George was a Roman soldier who came from Cappadocia. We were exploring the actual valley where the dragon was supposed to have had his lair and the legendary battle was fought and won.

Talking of battles, do you remember those Turkish wrestlers? They were the champions of Turkey and we went to meet them. We arrived just as they were emptying giant tins of salad oil over each other. That's what makes Turkish wrestling unique. Two slippery men in leather trousers try to get to grips with each other—and it's just about impossible. A bout takes ages, so it's just as well that a band plays all the time, otherwise it could get rather boring!

When the country's championships take place hundreds of wrestlers take part. They all wrestle at the same time and the matches carry on till there's only one pair left. The last man on his feet becomes the Grand Champion of Turkey— and judging by the practice bout we watched, it's no easy title to earn!

The Turks have a great reputation as fighting men. In the days of the Sultans, the crack troops were called janissaries. Fanatically brave and prepared to fight to the death, they were feared by all who faced them. The original janissaries were captured Christian slaves taken as children and trained by their new masters to kill or be killed. They were the first soldiers in the world to be led by a full band. Their drums and songs terrified their enemies and many a crusader fled just at the sight of their relentless march! We saw that march when the last survivors of the janissaries, the ceremonial Mehter band, played specially for us. They looked tremendous. They still wear huge head-dresses, chain-mail, and carry glistening weapons.

We danced, too, and our partners were two of the strongest men in Turkey, contestants in the National Wrestling Championships.

We saw a practice bout. The slippery champions were covered in olive oil and had a job coming to grips!

But today there's no need to fear them. Their ferocious moustaches turned out to be stuck on with glue and they were as friendly and welcoming as all the other Turks we met on our Expedition. It's a great place and although we explored non-stop, we only scratched the surface of this extraordinary country.

I WAS A SAGGAR MAKER'S BOTTOM KNOCKER

[I wasn't really—I just wanted to say it!]

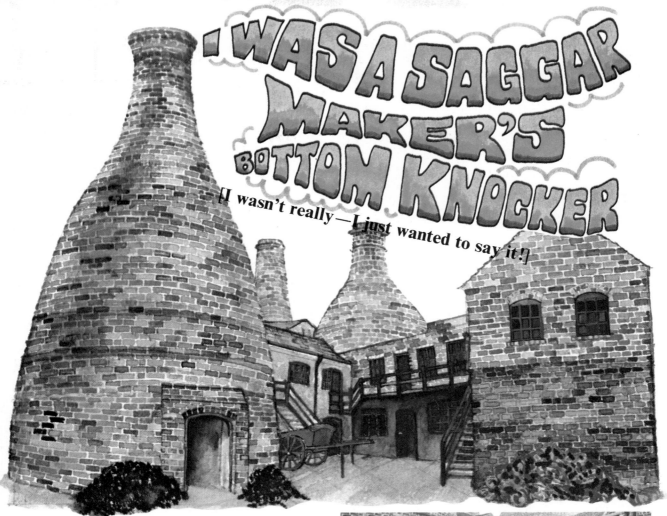

But I did find out what a Saggar was when I spent a day at Gladstone Pottery Museum in Longton, Stoke-on-Trent.

The huge bottle ovens used to dominate the landscape of the area known simply as the five towns. Tunstall, Burslem, Hanley, Stoke and Longton owe their existence and their wealth to the acrid smoke that used to belch from these oven chimneys and blacken the surrounding countryside.

Pottery is still made in the five towns but today the ovens are all fired by electricity and the towns are cleaner and better places because of it. But there's something romantic and magnificent about those massive bottle ovens and at the old Gladstone Pottery that grandeur has been preserved in a living Pottery Museum. I was able to try my hand at turning the great iron wheel that revolved the potter's wheel for David Rook. I got a bit bored with it after a while and David got a bit sharp with me when I turned too quickly or too slowly. The wrong speed could easily ruin the shape of the pot that was rising under his hands. I could fancy myself as a potter, but the thought of cranking the wheel round for twelve hours a day and being shouted at when I got it wrong, made me feel glad I wasn't a lad in the Stoke of 100 years ago

In the yard of the Gladstone Pottery Museum in Longton, Stoke-on-Trent.

I examined some of the pieces that had made the Gladstone Pottery famous throughout the world.

I turned the iron wheel that revolved the potter's wheel for craftsman David Rook.

I wouldn't have minded being a potter, but cranking that wheel all day long must have been no joke.

Fiddly painting isn't exactly my line, but all the age-old designs are faithfully reproduced.

Then I put a roll in my cap and braced myself for the lift.

But pottery isn't all made on the wheel. Some of it is made in moulds like Toby jugs and pigeons, cottages and dogs. And even more elaborate are the flower arrangements that have always been Gladstone specialities. Doris Kidney, who's worked in the Potteries since she was 13, gave me a lesson in rose making. She was very kind about my efforts, but compared with hers, my roses were more like cabbages.

When all the pots had been shaped and moulded by craftsmen, they were taken away to be fired, and that's when the saggar and bottle oven and the black, black smoke came in.

The bottle ovens were in use until only 15 years ago. They burned 10 tons of coal to fire each ton of pottery, and the men in charge had to work through the day and night. Their families brought food to keep them going because firing could take $2\frac{1}{2}$ days, and if anything went wrong a whole week's production could be ruined.

But before the firing started, the bottle oven had to be filled with pottery. Obviously, you couldn't just fling in cups and saucers, dogs and flower arrangements any old how. They all had to be stacked in special containers and these containers were called—wait for it—SAGGARS! (Just for the record, a saggar maker was the man who made the saggar, and his bottom knocker wasn't there to punish him, but to make up the base of the saggar.)

The saggars were filled with pots and carried on the heads of workmen with special "rolls"

I went inside the great bottle oven and began to load up my saggar with pots.

With the saggar balanced on my head I began to stack the oven.

It used to take five days to fill a single oven which would take up to 4000 saggars.

Every saggar has a special place because some pots need more heat than others.

Once the oven was full, the door was bricked up and the firing began.

This was my presentation plate.

It was a very proud moment for me when, on behalf of Blue Peter, I was invited to cut the tape and declare the Gladstone Pottery Museum Centre well and truly open.

inside their caps to protect their heads. Then they were stacked on racks until the bottle ovens were full. An oven properly stacked could take 4000 saggars but the placing required a special skill because some pots needed more heat than others. It took five days to fill an oven and then the door was bricked up and the firing began. The flames would roar through the furnace until the heat reached temperatures of 1300 degrees. Thick black smoke swirled round the saggars and out of the hole in the roof. Outside, the men watched the raging inferno through narrow peepholes set in the brickwork.

But when the burning was over, they couldn't wait for the oven to cool down. Time was money in the Potteries, and as soon as the fire was out, the workers were in, rushing across the burning floor with wet sacks wrapped round their hands and heads to protect them from the scorching saggars.

The Gladstone Pottery in its heyday had sent examples of British pottery all over the world, so many of its pieces are now collectors' items. I, for one, am pleased that modern technology has taken some of the boredom and dirt and misery away from the pottery workers. But I'm glad that the Gladstone Pottery Museum has been preserved as a living legend of the past. Not just something to be looked at, but a place with a special centre where people can come to classes to learn how to make the pots that have been famous for more than a century. You can understand that it was a proud moment for me when I was asked to a ceremony at which, accompanied by a brass band with the bottle ovens draped in bunting, I declared the Gladstone Pottery Museum Centre well and truly open.

BLEEP & BOOSTER

Miron City was stricken and helpless. Spaceships lay like stranded whales— powerless and silent. The domes and towers were plunged in darkness, and in the murk, little groups of Mirons huddled together for warmth and comfort.

"If it goes on like this much longer," grumbled Booster, "I'm rocketing back to Earth."

"I see," snapped Bleep, the Space boy. "You're following the old Earth sayings. You're going to be a rat leaving a sinking ship!"

The cause of all the misery was the sudden dwindling and all but disappearance of the source of Miron City's power, the strange rock Energon that was mined to give them light and fuel. It should have lasted for ever, but all at once, supplies had run short till now the little Energon that was left could only be used sparingly to light the Space Commando headquarters and keep just one fleet of ships in patrol. At that moment they were out on a desperate search to track down a new Energon field, and in command was Bleep's father, the captain. To escape the gloom, Bleep, Booster and his little space dog Fido, had wandered away from the City—but it hadn't worked. They were jumpy and quarrelsome.

"You're just a fair weather friend," continued

Bleep bitterly. "At the first hint of trouble you're . . ."

At that moment there was a rumble beneath their feet; then a shattering crack, and in a second the earth split beneath them and they crashed into a headlong fall.

Shaken and frightened, it took the two boys a few moments to take stock of the situation. They weren't hurt, and Fido, too, had landed safely. They appeared to have landed in a sort of cavern, dark and echoing, and far, far above them was a faint gleam of light from the crack through which they'd fallen.

"We can't get back," whispered Booster, after a valiant attempt to scramble up the cavern walls.

"The rock's too sheer and I can't get a hold."

"I'll try," said Bleep bravely, but even with his suction feet to help him, he couldn't get a grip on the glassy surface and soon he, too, fell back to join his friend.

"Now what," queried Bleep, his quarrel with Booster all forgotten. "What are we going to do?"

"Cheer up," cried Booster. "You've got your radio transmitter. Just give your Dad a buzz and the Commandos will get us out of here in no time! They've never let us down yet. And while we're waiting, I'll share out my emergency ration pack!"

Booster tipped out from the lightweight pack some Meteormeat sandwiches, a bottle of Gravity Pop and a packet of Gamma Gum drops. He was so busy sharing the goodies with Fido that he didn't notice the desperate look on Bleep's face, as he fiddled desperately with the controls on his

transmitter and tried time after time to make contact with the outside world.

"Bleep and Booster to Miron Control. Can you hear me? Come in Miron Control."

Bleep's desperate calls got louder and louder, and with a shock, Booster realised that help was not coming after all! Once more the two friends were in a life and death situation.

"What's wrong?" he asked calmly, swallowing his fears. "Was your radio smashed when you fell?"

"Not that I can see," replied Bleep. "It's some sort of interference. There's nothing but crackles, and I can't think why! And if no one can hear us, we'll never get out of here!"

"Oh don't give up," said Booster comfortingly. "Have a sandwich and we'll try and think of a plan." But by the time the boys had finished eating no brain-wave had struck them. By now it was dark outside and the light coming through the crack above them had vanished.

"If we can't go back," said Bleep bravely, "we'll just have to go on. I'll lead the way."

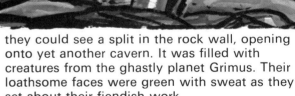

they could see a split in the rock wall, opening onto yet another cavern. It was filled with creatures from the ghastly planet Grimus. Their loathsome faces were green with sweat as they set about their fiendish work.

"They're Grimaloids," cried Bleep in horror.

Booster agreed, and with Fido tucked under one arm and his emergency ration pack under the other he followed his friend down the tunnel.

They fumbled their way for what seemed hours, and then, as they rounded a corner they saw a faint purple glow in the distance. Was there someone else in this ghastly place?

Bleep and Booster clutched at each other in horror. They could hear faint clinking sounds, but what could possibly be lurking in these depths?

"There's only one way to find out," whispered Bleep. "Let's go and investigate."

As they crept closer to the light, the sounds got louder. Voices mingled with the grinding of machines and as they crept further into the tunnel

"They're our deadly enemies and they're mining!"

"And look *what* they're mining. Our Energon!" gasped Booster. He stretched his arm through the gap and broke off a violet-coloured glowing lump.

"No wonder your radio wouldn't work, Bleep. There's enough power down here to cause interference to a set a hundred times more powerful!"

Quickly the boys pulled back into the darkness and tried to assess the situation. Terrified though they were, they set about it methodically.

"One," said Bleep, through chattering teeth, "there *is* another Energon field—and the Grimaloid invaders have found it first."

"Two," added Booster, "we've got to warn the Captain. And that means getting out."

"Three," said Bleep desperately, "we can't!" "Oh dear!" he wailed, "what shall we do? Those Grimaloids will kill us if they catch us!"

"We'll have to go on," cried Booster. They fumbled their way deeper and deeper into the darkness until a hideous sound stopped them dead in their tracks. As they clung together in the dark they became aware of a ghastly rasping. It wasn't from the mine, but from somewhere ahead.

They stopped in horror as the snorting turned to a roar. Two scarlet eyes were staring at them from a head full of teeth which topped a gigantic scaly body.

Fido leaped from Booster's arm whiffling with terror. Like a dart, he shot back along the tunnel towards the Grimaloid mine. After him lurched a slavering monster and as the two boys pressed themselves against the rock, they could feel its hot breath searing them as it lumbered past. There was a crash, a thump, then silence.

"Oh Fido," moaned Bleep. "That thing will have finished him off!"

"I'm going after him," yelled Booster. With Bleep hot on his heels, the boys dashed back. What they saw was extraordinary! The huge monster lay writhing in its death throes, its head and neck jammed tightly in the rift that lead to the mine. Fido was jumping round the cumbersome body snapping at its twitching tail, and as the boys thankfully snatched him up, the monster gave one last lurch—and died.

"Fido must have dashed into the mine and then doubled back when the monster's head poked through after him! Clever dog!" cried Booster.

"And its body's completely sealed the mine!

Those Grimaloids can't touch us now—and what's more, they're stuck in there until the Space Commandos round them up!"

The boys laughed delightedly. For a moment they'd forgotten they were stuck too, but as the realisation struck them once more, green tears rolled down Bleep's face.

"Cheer up," said Booster kindly. "Let's go back to the entrance and have one more try at scaling the walls."

He knew as well as Bleep that there was no possibility of climbing to safety, but as he walked back, comforting his friend, an idea was going round and round in Booster's head.

Back at the entrance, things looked just as bad. The gap was high above them—but at least it was still there.

"Look," said Booster, "are you sure your radio won't work?"

"Yes," gulped Bleep.

"Then rip all the cable leads off and let me have them."

Mystified, Bleep did as he was asked. At the same time, Booster got out his ration pack and tipped all the food on the ground!

"Have you gone mad?" Bleep cried.

"No, but we don't need any because we'll be out of here in no time, thanks to Fido!"

As he spoke, Booster had tied one end of each cable to the corners of his light-weight pack and tied the loose ends round the empty sandwich box.

"What's that for?" queried Bleep. "It looks like a sort of a parachute."

"This isn't going down," cried Booster. "It's going up! It's my version of earth man's first flying machine. It's a hot air balloon—and Fido's going up!"

Quickly he put the lump of Energon in the box and popped Fido on top with an SOS message. To Bleep's amazement the bag inflated, powered by the Energon lump, and Fido floated gracefully upwards and out through the crack.

"I do like dogs," said Booster as he settled down to wait. "They're man's best friends."

"And spaceman's!" laughed Bleep a few minutes later as they heard the roar of a rescuing spaceship overhead. "Thanks to him we've caught the Grimaloids and discovered a new mine. Fido may be little, but he's packed with power!"

This monument to the sailors of *H.M.S. Anson* recalls a fearful shipwreck **169** years ago.

Henry Trengrouse and the other Cornishmen struggled to reach the shipwrecked sailors who were only 100 yards from the shore.

Captain Lydiard tried to carry the Midshipman to safety, but they perished with 100 more seamen.

On Bonfire night, Trengrouse had a wonderful idea for saving life at sea whilst he was watching the fireworks.

He invented a safety rocket that could carry a lifeline to a ship in danger.

> Sacred to the memory of about 100 officers and men of *H.M.S. Anson* who were drowned when this ship was wrecked on Loe Bar, 29th December, 1807, and buried hereabout.
> Henry Trengrouse of Helston was so impressed by this tragedy that he invented the life saving rocket apparatus which has since been instrumental in saving thousands of lives.
> Erected March 1949.

A white cross, bearing this inscription, stands on the Cornish cliffs near Porthleven, Britain's most southerly port. Five miles away lies the ancient town of Helston.

I was mystified by the monument—I know the Cornish coast is treacherous, with gale force winds and powerful currents waiting to drive ships on to the jagged rocks. Every inch of the Cornish coast has tales to tell of good ships wrecked, and brave seamen drowned.

But the view from the monument seems calm and peaceful, with a long sandy beach stretching away to the west. What disaster had happened here?

I set out to trace the *Anson*'s story.

I discovered that, below the cliffs, there is a freshwater lake, divided from the turbulent sea by a bank of sand, called Loe Bar. As deadly as any rocks, this hidden sand was the cause of a terrible shipwreck.

H.M.S. Anson was a sixty-four-gun frigate of the Royal Navy. On Christmas Eve, 1807, she sailed from Falmouth, about twenty miles from Porthleven, with three hundred men on board. Britain was at war with France, and the *Anson* was to take part in the blockade of Brest, in Brittany.

Within a couple of days, she ran into appalling south-westerly gales. Blustering wind and driving rain met her head on, forcing her off course. Captain Lydiard, her captain, tried to thrust forward, but it was impossible.

Battered and helpless, the ship put back to port. On 29th December, after five ghastly days, she had almost reached the shelter of Porthleven harbour.

The seamen tried to drop anchor and ride out the storm, but the winds forced the ship further and further inshore, until she was driven aground on the hidden sands of Loe Bar.

She could not put to sea again, and was likely to be battered to pieces between the driving wind and pounding waves. Then, as she was driven over on her side, her mainmast was jammed firm between the rocks. She was absolutely helpless, but strangely enough, the mast made a kind of bridge and some seamen tried to escape. Many fell, to perish in the swirling waters, but those who got to the rocks managed to scramble ashore.

As news of the ship's plight spread, hundreds of Cornishmen poured out from Porthleven and nearby Helston. They gathered, helpless, on the shore, for no boat could put out in that boiling, shallow sea.

Mr Roberts, a brave citizen of Helston, tied a rope round his waist, and swam out to the wreck, while strong men on shore held the other end. He made his rope fast, and clinging to it, some sailors managed to get ashore. It saved lives, but it was desperately risky, and Mr Roberts himself was nearly drowned.

His struggles were watched by another Helston man—Henry Trengrouse, wishing passionately there was some way of making safe contact between ship and shore.

At last, only Captain Lydiard was left aboard. When he was certain that all the ship's company had left, and that nothing could be done for the ship, he prepared to brave the precarious mast bridge.

At the last second, he heard a sound which came from a rain-drenched bundle of rags. It was Richard Leech, Midshipman, who had been too terrified to move. He was only eleven years old.

Captain Lydiard turned back, slung the boy over his shoulder and tried to make the crossing.

It was impossible to balance.

He slipped—and fell!

Captain and Midshipman were both drowned between ship and shore, within sight of hundreds of would-be rescuers.

At daybreak the hundred and seventeen survivors were taken into homes in Porthleven and Helston, and treated kindly. Nearly a hundred bodies were recovered from the sea. They were buried in a field on the cliff top, with no kind of religious ceremony, and no kind of monument, until the memorial cross was put up, one hundred and forty-two years afterwards.

One man in Helston could not forget that dreadful December day when the *Anson* was lost. Henry Trengrouse was determined to work to prevent such tragedies.

He was a cabinet-maker, with a prosperous business, so tools, wood, skill and money were all to hand as he tried to forge a link between ship and shore, but none of his ideas worked.

Then one Bonfire Night, he took his children to watch the fireworks on Helston Green.

In a flash, he found the answer—rockets!

Next day he was on the Green measuring to see how far rockets travelled, and what they could carry. He went to the beach at Porthleven, the scene of the wreck, and constructed a rocket that could carry a lifeline from ship to shore, or from shore to a ship in trouble.

He had found the solutions—would shipowners adopt it?

The Royal Navy seemed interested, so Henry Trengrouse demonstrated his lifeline at Woolwich, on the River Thames, to an admiral. He was impressed, and promised the navy would order fifty sets, to be made by Henry Trengrouse in his workshop.

He certainly hoped for some recompense; he had spent years of his life, and £3,000 of his own money, developing his rocket. But all he got was a letter from the Admiralty, telling him they would make their own version of the safety rocket. They sent Trengrouse £50 for his trouble!

Oddly enough, he did receive one award—sent to him by the Tsar of Russia. He had heard of Trengrouse's work, so he sent him a diamond ring —all the way from Russia to Cornwall.

Trengrouse died in 1854, almost unknown. He is buried in Helston, and in the town there is a street named Trengrouse Way, but few people even there know much about him. One of the *Anson's* guns, brought from the wreck, stands outside the Guildhall, but Henry's original rocket hangs unnoticed in the town's museum.

Yet sailors say that in the last hundred years, more than ten thousand lives have been saved by the safety rocket.

The dangerous seas, not only round Cornwall, but all over the world, have been made safer because of Henry Trengrouse, and the lifeline he pioneered.

Perhaps that is the memorial he would have wished for!

Stick your favourite cartoon character all round a home-made belt and you can follow the fashion and have a laugh while you're doing it!
To make the belt, you'll need an old buckle and a piece of webbing or strong material long enough to go round your waist with about 20 centimetres to spare. As well as that, you'll want some transparent sticky-backed plastic and about four picture strips cut from a comic. I've chosen Mickey Mouse. I wonder what you'll choose?

1 Cut one end of your webbing to a neat point. Starting at the pointed end, glue your first cartoon strip carefully to the webbing. Fold the extra bit of comic strip over the point and glue it to the back of the belt for a neat finish. When you've done that, go on glueing cartoon strips until the webbing is covered. To go round me, I need four strips of three pictures.

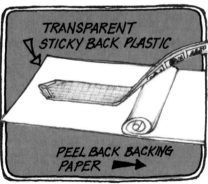

TRANSPARENT STICKY BACK PLASTIC

PEEL BACK BACKING PAPER ➤

2 To cover the belt, you'll need a sheet of transparent sticky-backed plastic slightly longer than the webbing, and about $2\frac{1}{2}$ times as wide. Lay the plastic shiny side down and peel a little of the backing paper away. Press the belt picture side down in the middle of the plastic, gradually peeling off the backing paper as you go. When you've covered the whole of the front of the belt, fold the rest of the plastic over to cover the back and neaten the join with a pair of scissors.

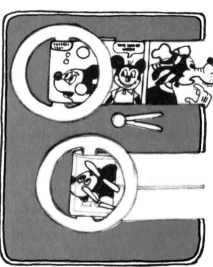

3 Thread the straight edge of your cartoon belt through the buckle and fasten with brass paper clips. You'll probably need to make some holes first. Finish off your belt by sticking a piece of sticky plastic over the pointed ends of the paper fasteners, just to make sure they don't tear your clothes!

CLOTHES HORSE RACE

We couldn't get the day we spent with Stephen, Peter, Debbie, Judy, Johnny, Titch, and all the other disabled riders out of our minds. Surely there was *something* we could do so that more badly handicapped people could join groups like the one we visited?

We did some research. And we discovered that a lot of classes had waiting lists because there was such a shortage of suitable ponies and equipment.

That's how our Clothes Horse Race began. If only we could collect 200 tons of old wool and cotton, we could provide and train a pony *and* supply equipment to more than 300 groups for handicapped riders all over Britain.

In the past, we'd always received such fantastic help from Blue Peter viewers, we thought we *might* be able to reach that 200-ton Target. But with postal charges even higher than ever, we knew we could be asking the impossible.

We hadn't counted on two things. Another marvellous offer of nationwide free delivery from BRS Parcels (Ltd.) and the determination of 8 million Blue Peter viewers.

Your parcels bombarded our Collecting Depot at such a rate, we'd reached the 200-ton target by 1st January 1976.

These huge bobbins were amongst the 800 tons of old wool and cotton sent to our Clothes-Horse Race Depot.

All the rags were sorted at a factory and then reprocessed. Our Appeal was helping conservation, too!

It was quite unbelievable! And it was a very moving moment when we not only filled our studio to overflowing with all the equipment your old rags had provided, but when we were able to lead in our trainee pony for handicapped riders.

She was a very sturdy 5 years old. A breed called Connemara—and veterinary experts said she was perfect for the job.

During the next seven days, more than 58,000 postcards arrived with suggestions for her name—and by popular—and highly appropriate—vote she was called Rags.

At the end of her year's training with one of the country's top instructors, Tessa Martin-Bird, we hope Rags will pass her tests and become a fully qualified pony for handicapped riders. She certainly shows every sign of doing so at the moment.

But that wasn't all. Reaching our 200-ton Target by

1st January was just the beginning of the good news. By the end of February we'd *quadrupled* it with a total of 800 tons!

As well as that, apart from all the old rags you sent, there were some superb antiques and garments that were real collectors' items. These went to a public auction at Phillips, and all the wearable garments went to our Jumble Sale at Petticoat Lane.

Altogether, our Clothes-Horse Race results stand at:
Rags plus 20 other ponies for disabled riders.
Equipment for 300 handicapped riding groups.
An Indoor Riding School at Tyne and Wear.
10 Field Shelters.
16 Tack Rooms.
20 Wheelchair ramps.

After all that, we can only say "thank you" to every single person who helped—and declare our Clothes-Horse Race well and truly won!

1 Rags, Blue Peter's trainee pony for disabled riders, is being taught by one of Britain's top instructors, Tessa Martin-Bird. After only $3\frac{1}{2}$ months Rags had made tremendous progress and in April, Princess Anne came to the stables to give Rags her first important test.

2 Breaking in a pony has to be taken in easy stages. Here Rags gets used to a rider leaning over her.

3 Rags' first big test was being ridden for the first time ever off the lunge rein. Princess Anne was the rider and Rags passed the test with flying colours!

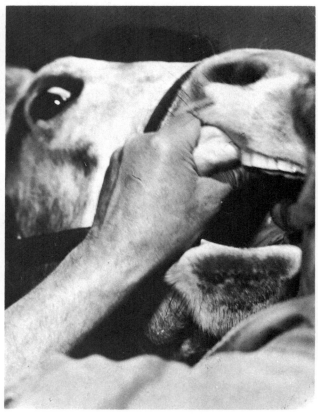

4 Dental hygiene applies to horses as well as humans! Rags behaved very well when she had her teeth scaled by veterinary surgeon Alan Berry.

Story by Michael Bond illustrated by "Hargreaves"

PADDINGTON IN THE HOT SEAT

HAPPINESS IS MARMILADE

A POT OF WHAT?

VINTG MARMILADE

Paddington sat up in bed, and after peering at his reflection in a glass of water, ran a comb carefully through his whiskers. Then he wrapped a scarf round his neck, broke the end off a bar of chocolate, and dipped it into a newly opened jar of his favourite marmalade. That completed, he absent-mindedly began stirring a mug of cocoa with the end of a felt-tipped pen while he peered at an important-looking envelope lying unopened on his breakfast tray.

It was Christmas morning, and he was suffering from his usual attack of not knowing which of his many presents to test first.

One of the nice things about living with the Browns was that the opening of presents was made to go on for as long as possible. Apart from having mounds of parcels round the tree, Paddington was always

allowed to hang a pillow-case at the foot of his bed, and when he woke he usually found he'd mysteriously acquired a small stockingful of goodies into the bargain as well.

This year had been no exception, and apart from the parcels he'd already opened there was this very special envelope. It bore the crest of the British Broadcasting Corporation, and across the back, in bold letters, were the words NOT TO BE OPENED UNTIL CHRISTMAS DAY!

Paddington had never received a Christmas present from the BBC before and he grew more and more excited as he tore open the envelope and a large card fell out.

His eyes grew larger and larger as he took in the wording, and soon the whole household was in an

sounded very good value indeed—especially the bit about having two bites of a cherry.

Paddington was up bright and early the next morning, and he spent most of the day poring over Mr Brown's encyclopedias so that he could take full advantage of his outing.

"I do hope he'll be all right," said Mrs Brown

uproar as he hurried downstairs in order to tell the others.

"Gosh!" said Judy enviously, "an invitation to see SAGE OF BRITAIN! It's a special early evening Boxing Day edition as well."

"What a nice way to round off Christmas," broke in Mrs Brown.

"There's a message on the back of the card," exclaimed Jonathan. "It's from the BLUE PETER office, and it looks like John's writing. 'Best wishes for Christmas! Hope to see you there.' Peter and Lesley have signed it as well!"

"I wonder how they knew Paddington likes quiz programmes?" remarked Mr Brown.

"They're the sort who leave no stone unturned when they want to find out something," said Mrs Bird mysteriously. "They must have made some enquiries."

The Browns' housekeeper approved of BLUE PETER. Over the years they had been very kind to Paddington; apart from that it kept him quiet every Monday and Thursday afternoon when he sat glued to the screen while he followed the fortunes of the team.

However, undoubtedly the second favourite programme at number thirty-two Windsor Gardens was SAGE OF BRITAIN.

SAGE OF BRITAIN was a quiz show in which each contestant had two bites of the cherry as it were. First they had to answer questions on a subject of their choice, then they had to talk for a further three minutes on another subject. The one who got the most votes from viewers at the end of the series was pronounced the winner and awarded the title of CHIEF SAGE for the year.

Although Paddington liked quiz programmes, he'd never actually seen SAGE OF BRITAIN as it usually came on after he'd gone to bed. However, when the others explained the rules he decided it

anxiously as he set off in a taxi soon after tea. "I never like him going out by himself after it gets dark —especially on Boxing Day."

"Perhaps we shall see him on the screen," said Judy. "They often have shots of the audience."

"I shouldn't worry yourselves," said Mrs Bird. "I spoke to the BLUE PETER office on the phone only the other day and they promised they would see him safely home. Besides, he knows enough people at the Television Centre."

In saying Paddington knew lots of people at the BBC, Mrs Bird was making something of an understatement. Through his many visits to the BLUE PETER studio he'd become a familiar figure with the staff. The result was that as soon as he showed his head round the door of the entrance hall people started rushing up to greet him.

What with one thing and another it wasn't until a few minutes before the programme was due to start that he suddenly realised the time, and he had to say some very rapid goodbyes indeed before hurrying off in search of the studio.

On the face of it the BBC Television Centre was a very simple building. It was shaped like a giant hollow cake, with all the studios radiating out from the bottom floor, joined to each other by layers of circular corridors.

The only trouble was that if you set off in the wrong direction you could easily end up with twice as far to go and it certainly took twice as long, which was why, when Paddington at last reached the right studio, he saw to his dismay that the red light was already on.

Pushing open the heavy sound-proof door he found himself in a darkened area of the studio.

"Sorry, mate," said a stalwart commissionaire, barring his way. "I'm afraid you can't come in once the programme's started."

"I can't come in!" exclaimed Paddington. He looked most upset as he peered at the man through the gloom. "But I've got a special invitation *and* I've spent all day studying Mr Brown's encyclopedias!"

It was the commissionaire's turn to look bothered. "My mistake, sir," he hissed, touching his cap as a mark of respect. "I didn't realise who you were. Come this way at once—then I'll let the Producer know you're here."

SAGE OF BRITAIN attracted many famous contestants to the portals of the BBC. Over the years some of the best brains in Britain had taken part, and as was so often the case beauty didn't always go hand in hand with brains.

"All the same," whispered the commissionaire to a friend as he ushered Paddington into a small room at the side of the studio, "I reckon he takes the cake. He couldn't have been in the front rank when inches was handed out."

"I expect all the goodness went into his brains," whispered his colleague. "Did you see all them whiskers? Probably some kind of professor. Very erudite if you ask me."

The second commissionaire wasn't the only one to have taken note of Paddington's appearance.

Once inside the room Paddington found himself confronted by a girl in blue striped overalls, who sat him down in front of a mirror. She picked up a comb and eyed his reflection doubtfully as she helped him off with his hat.

"Do you part your fur in the middle?" she asked.

"I *never* part with my fur," said Paddington firmly. "I've had it ever since I was born."

"I didn't mean that," said the girl hastily. "It's just that I've never made up a bear before and I'm not quite sure what to do."

"We normally put some powder on the forehead," she explained, "but yours is a bit er . . . um . . ."

"My forehead's a bit er . . . um?" exclaimed Paddington hotly. "But I washed it specially this morning."

"Oh dear," said the girl. She broke off as the door suddenly opened and two men wearing headphones came into the room.

"Sorry about this," said the first man. "I didn't realise we had another candidate." He hung a small microphone round Paddington's neck and then bent down to speak into it. "One . . . two . . . three . . . testing. Good . . . now you try saying something."

"'Something'," said Paddington dutifully.

"I didn't mean 'something'," said the man. "I meant 'anything'."

Paddington gave the man a hard stare. He rather wished he would make up his mind. "Anything," he said.

The engineer looked at him wearily and then decided to have one last try. "Tell us what you had for breakfast this morning," he suggested.

Paddington looked most surprised. "I had some

chocolate," he announced. "Then I had bacon and eggs, and two mugs of cocoa, and toast and marmalade, and some sausages Mrs Bird had left over from the Christmas Dinner . . ." He bent down and opened his suitcase. "I've still got one or two left if you're hungry."

The others exchanged glances. "Ask a silly question," said the first engineer. He listened to his headphones for a moment and then took a closer look at Paddington. "You may have to have your whiskers trimmed," he announced. "We're picking up a lot of crackles. These microphones are very sensitive, you know."

"So are my whiskers!" exclaimed Paddington hotly.

"Perhaps you could use the ends in a crystal set," broke in the second engineer jokingly. "You know—like they did with cats-whiskers in the old days."

Paddington jumped up in alarm. "Use the ends of my whiskers in a crystal set!" he exclaimed in alarm. "I don't think Auny Lucy would like that!"

He was about to explain that he wouldn't like it very much either, but fortunately for all concerned there was yet another interruption as a harassed-looking man wearing headphones and clutching a clip-board suddenly rushed into the room.

"Terribly sorry," he said, holding out his hand. "Ronnie's the name—call me Ron. I'm the studio manager. Didn't have your name on my list. Nobody tells me *anything*! There's not a moment to lose— you're on next." And before Paddington had a chance to say anything more he found himself being propelled at high speed through a maze of cables and wires, round the back of some sets and past some cameras, to where the audience was sitting.

The studio manager paused in order to give the signal for some applause, then he pointed Paddington in the direction of a platform on which a single chair stood bathed in the harsh glare of a spotlight.

"Quick," he hissed, giving Paddington a push.

"You're in the 'hot seat'!"

Paddington raised his hat to the audience several times and then hurried on to the platform. So much had happened in a short space of time he didn't know whether he was coming or going, but he didn't at all like the sound of the latest development, so he bent down in order to make sure the chair was safe to sit on.

"It's all right, Ron," he called, turning to wave at the studio manager. "I think it's cooled down now."

If Lionel Pear, the questionmaster, was taken aback by Paddington's sudden appearance he was much too experienced to show more than the merest flicker.

"Do take your duffel coat off," he said, hurriedly sorting through some cards on his desk. "You may find it a trifle warm under the lights."

"I don't think I will, thank you, Mr Pear," said Paddington. "I shan't feel the benefit afterwards if I do. Mrs Bird wouldn't like that."

Lionel Pear took a closer look at Paddington. "All right," he said grudgingly, "but do you *have* to bring your suitcase with you?"

"Yes," said Paddington firmly.

Lionel Pear gave a defeated sigh.

"May I have my points, please," said Paddington.

"Your *points?*" repeated the questionmaster in a daze. "What points?"

"Well, you asked me a question, Mr Pear," said Paddington, "and I got it right. You asked me if I had to have my suitcase with me and I do. I've got my sausages in it."

"Hear! Hear!" called a familiar voice in the audience.

"Certainly not," said Lionel Pear with a touch of petulance in his voice. "We haven't started yet." He took a deep breath and then turned and beamed at one of the other cameras. The programme had been going particularly smoothly until a moment ago, but now a nasty doubt had crept into his mind. That was one of the troubles about a 'live' show—once you'd started there was no going back.

But if Lionel Pear was feeling anxious about the unusual turn of affairs, his viewing audience—or part of it watching the 'goings-on' from the safety of the dining-room at number thirty-two Windsor Gardens, was even more alarmed.

"What *is* that bear up to?" exclaimed Mrs Bird.

"I said we might see him on the screen," said Judy excitedly. "I didn't dream he'd actually be on the programme."

"Ssh!" broke in Jonathan. "They're about to start the questions."

"Are you sitting comfortably?" called the questionmaster, as Paddington climbed on to the chair and settled back.

"Yes, thank you, Mr Pear," said Paddington. He peered down at the microphone on his chest and gave it a hard blow. "Testing," he called in a loud voice. "One . . . two . . . three . . . testing."

A look of pain crossed Lionel Pear's face. "I suppose you realise," he exclaimed, "that you nearly blew my eardrums out!"

Picking up a small object from the table he put it back in his ear.

"I'm sorry, Mr Pear," said Paddington. "I didn't realise you were deaf."

"I am *not* deaf!" shouted Lionel Pear. "I wear this ear-piece so that the director can speak to me. Now, as you know, I shall be awarding ten points for each question you get right. What is your special subject?"

"Marmalade sandwiches," said Paddington promptly.

"*Marmalade sandwiches?*" The questionmaster tapped his ear-piece to make sure it hadn't been damaged when it fell out. "But I don't have any questions on marmalade sandwiches," he said plaintively.

"You could ask me where I can get some," said Paddington.

Lionel Pear riffled desperately through some more cards on his desk. "Well," he said, playing for time, "where *can* you get some?"

"I don't know," replied Paddington. "I was hoping you would tell me, Mr Pear."

He looked hopefully at the scoreboard.

"Is anything the matter?" asked the questionmaster.

"I was wondering if I could have my points now," said Paddington. "You asked me what my subject was, and I got that right. Then you couldn't answer my question about the sandwiches, so that's another ten for me."

Lionel Pear removed a handkerchief from his breast pocket and dabbed nervously at his forehead. "You're sure you haven't any more questions?" he enquired.

"Perhaps," said Paddington hopefully, "I could have my cherry now, Mr Pear?"

Although he'd done very well over Christmas, the lights were beginning to make him feel hungry again, and he hadn't even had one bite at the famous cherry so far, let alone the chance of a second one.

"I can't stand it," groaned Mr Brown. "Only Paddington would expect to get a *real* cherry."

"He's done jolly well," said Judy. She pointed to the television set where a picture of the scoreboard had now flashed on the screen. "He's got maximum points for the first half."

"I think it's because there weren't any questions," said Jonathan. "It's one of the rules—only they've never had to use it before."

The Browns turned their attention back to the set as Lionel Pear reappeared on the screen.

Obviously labouring under a great strain, Mr Pear had plunged into the second half and was questioning Paddington about television in general.

Taking a furtive glance at the studio clock he saw that there was still five minutes to go before the end of the programme. Never had the hands moved so slowly, and the way things were going five minutes might just as well have been five hours.

"Right," he said desperately, "you have three minutes to tell us what changes you would make if you were running the BBC."

Paddington settled back in his chair. He had very decided views on the subject and he felt it was much more up his street.

"To start with," he said, "I'd have lots more cookery programmes. I'd have a special series on marmalade and another one on cocoa."

"A series about cocoa?" repeated the questionmaster. "You can't have a whole series about cocoa."

"Mr Gruber's got lots of books about cocoa," said Paddington. You could even send an expedition out to South America to show where it comes from. And then you could have another programme all about getting the stains out.

"And I would have special sports programmes. There's lots about football and cricket, but there's never anything about important things like throwing snowballs. It's not very easy to do it properly— especially with paws.

"Then I'd have a special series for bears . . ."

"*Bears*?" Lionel Pear permitted himself a superior smile. "Don't you think that's something of a minority programme?"

"Not," said Paddington firmly, "if you happen to be a bear!"

"All very interesting," said Mr Pear hastily, as to his great relief he caught sight of the studio manager about to give the wind-up signal, "but scarcely practical. Who on earth would you get to look after all these programmes of yours?"

Paddington gave Lionel Pear a hard stare; one of his hardest ever. For someone who was supposed to be in charge of a quiz programme Mr Pear didn't seem to know very much.

"The BLUE PETER team, of course," he announced. "They can do anything.

"I'd put Mr Noakes in charge of cookery—some of his recipes are very good.

"Then I would put Miss Judd in charge of removing stains, and Mr Purves in charge of the bears' programme. He's very good with animals.

"In fact," he continued, making his final point, "if *I* was in charge of programmes I would make BLUE PETER last twice as long and I'd have it on *every* day."

Somewhere in the studio a suspiciously familiar voice called out "Hear! Hear!" and there was a burst of clapping which was rapidly taken up by the rest of the audience. In fact the applause went on for so long Lionel Pear had great difficulty in making himself heard. In any case, though, his attention was obviously taken up with other things as he pressed home his ear-piece and concentrated on some last-minute instructions coming from the gallery.

"Good Heavens!" he exclaimed. "Good gracious! Really?"

When Mr Pear at last turned his attention back to Paddington it was with a look of new respect on his face.

"I'm afraid," he said, "that because this is an extra holiday programme we can't count it as part of our regular series, but I've just been given some special instructions.

"It seems," he continued, "that you've jammed our switchboard."

Paddington jumped to his feet in alarm. "I've jammed your switchboard!" he exclaimed. "But I haven't been anywhere near it!"

Lionel Pear raised his hand to quell the buzz of excitement which ran round the studio. "It's been jammed," he explained dramatically, as the programme reached its final few seconds, "by thousands of Blue Peter viewers! They've all been phoning in to congratulate you on the best programme ideas they've heard for a long time, and by popular request it's my pleasure to name you CHRISTMAS SAGE of 1976!"

Paddington nearly fell over backwards with surprise at the news. "Thank you *very* much, Mr Pear," he exclaimed.

He considered the matter for a moment. Then, as the final credits began to roll across the screen, he came to a decision and opening his suitcase he produced a strange-looking object in silver foil. Unwrapping it, he held the contents up to the camera and then proffered it to the questionmaster.

"This is some special plum pudding Mr Noakes showed how to make last week," he announced. "It's the kind of thing you would have *every* day if I was ever put in charge, and it's a very good way to finish off a programme, especially a Christmas one when you've just been made a Sage!"

HARGREAVES

COUNTRY GIANT

It felt more like driving a tank than a tractor when I manoeuvred this 10½-tonne giant into the studio.

This giant tractor was one of the biggest vehicles we'd ever driven in the Blue Peter studio. It even dwarfed one of our Blue Peter cameras!

Star exhibit of the Royal Smithfield Show, it's the very latest thing in farm equipment. The only snag is, your farm needs to measure thousands, not hundreds, of acres!

Its vital statistics are very impressive. There's a 215-hp diesel engine, no less than twenty gears —16 forward and 4 reverse— and in top gear speeds of 20 mph. The eight huge wheels each have a diameter of 1.75 metres. But if you want to change the giant into a four-wheeler, it only takes an hour to remove the outer ones.

You can see from the details on the opposite page that apart from its capacity for ploughing 11 acres an hour, this giant tractor has plenty of gadgets to make life more pleasant for the ploughman. His music while he works can come from a stereophonic radio, *or* an eight-track tape player, and there are things like special food cupboards, a padded swivel seat, air-conditioning, and sound-proofing.

As you might imagine, these giants were first built for the vast multi-thousand acre farmlands of the USA and Canada. But there are now some being used in Britain and they must be doing a lot to raise the level of food production.

Peter's signals helped me with my manoeuvring. I felt a bit like a Concorde pilot coming in to land!

There's just one problem. As well as having a big farm, you need to be a very rich farmer to own a giant tractor like this—to buy one you'd need £23,300!

Key to numbers:

(1) The driving cab, called a "Sound-Gard Body", is specially designed for quietness and has a rounded front to deflect engine noise away from the driver, as well as being padded with sound-proofing material called (2) lead septum—an insulating material originally developed for use in space flights. Perched high up, the cab gives the driver an all-round view through tinted-glass windows to prevent sun glare, and low level windows (3) at the front give him a view of the ground ahead. Access is gained through a front-facing door (4). Inside the air is kept at a constant temperature by an air-conditioning unit (5). Opening side and rear windows (6) provide additional ventilation.

Inside the cab driver's swivel seat (7) is adjustable for his height and weight, and the padded armrests can be raised or lowered. (8) Insulated food storage box. (9) Radio and eight-track cassette player. All controls are within

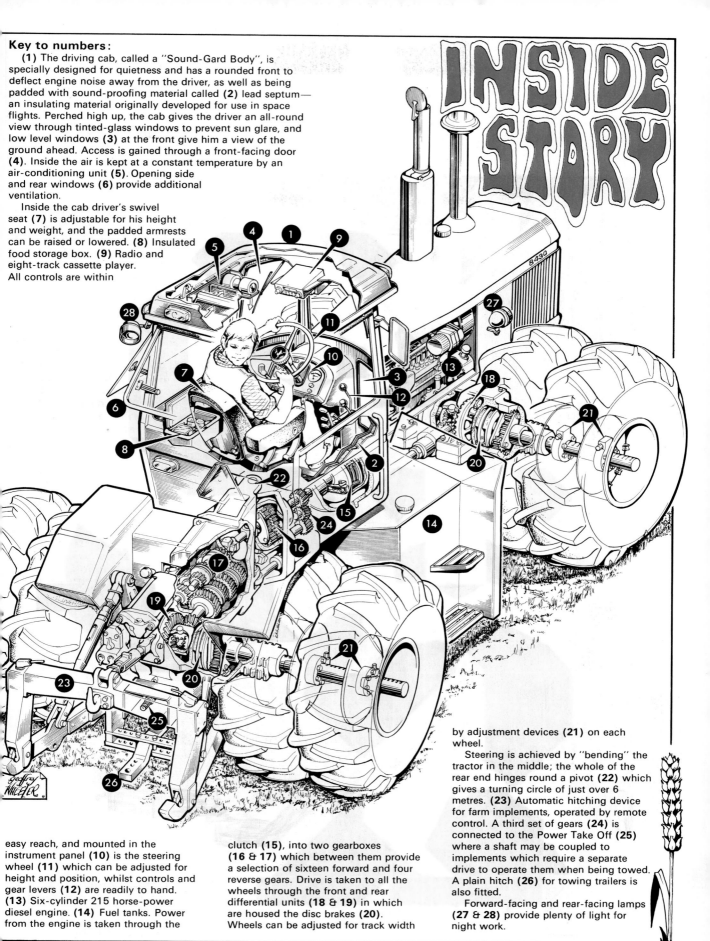

easy reach, and mounted in the instrument panel (10) is the steering wheel (11) which can be adjusted for height and position, whilst controls and gear levers (12) are readily to hand. (13) Six-cylinder 215 horse-power diesel engine. (14) Fuel tanks. Power from the engine is taken through the

clutch (15), into two gearboxes (16 & 17) which between them provide a selection of sixteen forward and four reverse gears. Drive is taken to all the wheels through the front and rear differential units (18 & 19) in which are housed the disc brakes (20). Wheels can be adjusted for track width

by adjustment devices (21) on each wheel.

Steering is achieved by "bending" the tractor in the middle; the whole of the rear end hinges round a pivot (22) which gives a turning circle of just over 6 metres. (23) Automatic hitching device for farm implements, operated by remote control. A third set of gears (24) is connected to the Power Take Off (25) where a shaft may be coupled to implements which require a separate drive to operate them when being towed. A plain hitch (26) for towing trailers is also fitted.

Forward-facing and rear-facing lamps (27 & 28) provide plenty of light for night work.

Mystery Picture

1. BLACK
2. BROWN
3. DARK BLUE
4. LIGHT BLUE
5. ORANGE
6. DARK GREEN
7. LIGHT GREEN
8. MAUVE
0. LEAVE WHITE

Colour the spaces as indicated by the
numbers and the mystery picture will appear.

STOWAWAYS!

Little did I know when I was given this dress from Senegal in West Africa that it was hiding two Stowaways!

Stowaway No. 1 was discovered when I brought the dress to the BBC's Wardrobe Department for some alterations. I wanted to wear it on the programme, but when the hem was cut open, out popped the most extraordinary-looking beetle— very much alive and none the worse for its 3,000-mile journey from Africa, plus two weeks in a plastic bag in my bedroom.

As far as we knew, the beetle could have been highly dangerous, so we sent it to the BBC's Medical Unit and had it examined by the BBC's doctor.

He'd never seen anything like it before, either. But he did a bit of research and discovered it was perfectly harmless, so we took the stowaway to the Natural History Museum, hoping *they'd* be able to solve the mystery—and they did. It was identified as a Golden Tortoise Beetle and it must have felt at home in the museum, because they literally have hundreds of them. But not alive. There's drawer after drawer of dead

Golden Tortoise Beetles, from over 40 different countries. Altogether there are about 150 different kinds. My Senegal beetle is about the size of a 10-pence piece. Part of its body is transparent, and part is gold coloured. It's so bright it actually flashes. And it changes colour, too, according to the temperature. That's why the museum was so delighted to have a live one —because after they're dead, of course, the beetles don't change colour, and the museum was anxious to take a series of photographs.

So that's how my unexpected new pet was lent to the museum where it's feeding on morning glory leaves and living in the lap of luxury. **P.S. Two days afterwards, Stowaway No. 2 was discovered in the BBC's Wardrobe Department! He'd obviously crawled out of my dress, too, so he's now joined his brother at the museum. But how many more have travelled to Britain in this way? For all we know, there's a whole colony of them living here at TV Centre!**

41

THE EGLINTON TOURNAMENT

Have you ever wanted to be a knight in shining armour? Back in the days of Queen Victoria, young Lord Eglinton did!

He hated the grim factories and noisy trains that were spreading over the country, and longed for the days of chivalry when knights were bold.

"I'll bring back the olden days," he said. "I'll hold a splendid tournament!" But he'd no idea what lay in store as he set out from Eglinton Castle at the head of a glittering band of Knights and Ladies.

Robert Broomfield

1 Lord Eglinton spent hours in his Scottish castle planning his Medieval Spectacular. "I don't care what it costs," he said. "I shall hold it next summer." Luckily, he was very rich.

2 He invited 150 friends to take part, and fitted them out with armour. They knew very little about jousting, and soon they were arguing hotly about what ought to happen. Some of them got so angry, they could hardly wait for the tournament to begin.

3 During the winter they all practised putting on their armour. They could hardly move—let alone joust! When they fell off their horses, they couldn't get up again. At the end of the dress rehearsal, only 13 knights agreed to take part in the actual tournament.

4 Meanwhile, back at Eglinton Castle, a vast arena was being prepared. Thrones were got ready for the King and Queen of the Tournament, grandstands were built for two thousand invited guests, and a huge tent was set up for them to have a medieval banquet after the jousting. But there was something Lord Eglinton hadn't planned for.

5 All over the country, people read about the Eglinton Tournament. "You shall go," fathers told their families. "It will make a nice outing." They hadn't been invited, but they weren't going to miss the treat!

6 They piled into the trains that Lord Eglinton hated so much and crammed on to the new steam passenger ferries that brought them within sight of Eglinton Castle.

7 Wednesday, 28 August 1838 was a lovely morning. The invited guests, dressed in their expensive medieval costumes, took their seats.

8 The uninvited guests found what space they could. To enter into the spirit of the thing they'd dressed up, too! Altogether, 100,000 people waited for the Grand Procession to begin. They had a long wait.

9 The knights couldn't get into their armour, the Queen of Beauty was never quite ready, and one knight couldn't get on to his horse. Only Lord Eglinton kept calm and unruffled.

10 At last everything was ready—just four hours late. Lord Eglinton gave the signal and the procession moved off. The Eglinton Tournament had begun.

CRASH—A clap of thunder! CRACK—A flash of lightning! Rain began to fall in buckets. The British Summer had done it once again! Horses slipped in the mud and weapons fell from the knights' frozen hands. Then the tent split and water cascaded on to rich costumes and elaborate hairdos. The uninvited guests huddled under their umbrellas, ankle deep in slush. Poor Lord Eglinton! He'd spent thousands of pounds. He'd made his friends wet and miserable. He'd disappointed thousands of people. The whole country would be laughing at him. Instead of a triumph, the Eglinton Tournament had ended up as Britain's biggest washout!

EVEREST MONSTERS

For hundreds of years there have been reports of a strange creature lurking on Mount Everest. It's said to be a hairy, shambling monster far bigger than a man—but no one has ever caught more than a fleeting glimpse of it.

Sometimes it's been called the Abominable Snowman and sometimes a Yeti. Some people think it walks on two feet, but others think it may bound along on all fours. It may be like a huge gorilla, or perhaps like some sort of bear. Maybe it even has wings and can fly! When we asked Blue Peter viewers what *they* thought Chris Bonington and his team might meet during their ascent of the south-west face of Mount Everest, we received 60,000 ideas. Here are the top prize-winning entries:

When we showed the paintings on the programme one of them caused a bit of a stir. We had five letters all saying the picture had been copied from a sketch in a book although one of the viewers who wrote to us said:
"Nevertheless, the adaptation was very well drawn and deserved a prize." And we agreed.
Although there were similarities, the competition painting had lots of original touches. For a start it was in colour and not black and white. There were a lot more mountains and all kinds of amusing ideas like the Union flag and the tent.

The black and white sketch on the left certainly looks similar to the painting on the right. But many great painters have adapted each other's works and you can see a couple of striking examples on the next page.

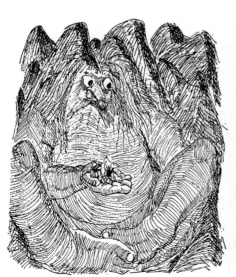

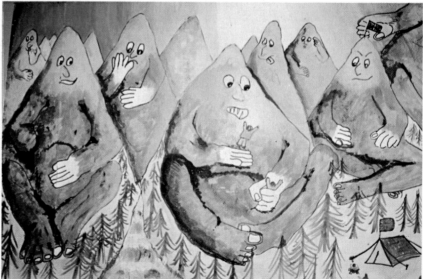

46

We were interested to discover that the adaptation of the sketch in the book followed a great tradition. Some of the world's greatest painters have got their ideas from each other's work. With these examples you can see how Van Gogh adapted a painting by Gustave Doré, and Pablo Picasso adapted a Velasquez that had been painted 300 years earlier.

Velasquez's painting with the little girls and the dog and the reflections in the mirror fascinated Picasso. He painted Las Meninas, too. And although you have to look quite hard to see them, the little girls, the dog and the mirror are all there—just as they are in the Velasquez—and what's more, he copied Las Meninas over and over again!

Las Meninas

Velasquez 1656

Pablo Picasso 1958

The Prison Court Yard

Gustave Doré 1872

Vincent Van Gogh 1890

It's a nice idea to feel that if you want to paint a picture and you can't think what to draw, it's the tradition to follow in the footsteps of the famous.

If you "borrow" a good idea, you don't have to make an exact copy—like Picasso and Van Gogh, you can turn it into a personal picture of your own.

THE FLAG THAT WENT TO EVEREST

The Blue Peter flags were amongst the final items to be loaded for the 1975 Everest Expedition.

Dougal Haston, one of the first men to get up Everest the hard way.

The other one—Doug Scott. The two men stood together on the roof of the world as the sun set on September 24th.

Mick Burke, the cameraman who tragically died making another assault on the summit.

When Chris Bonington, the leader of the British Everest Expedition, came to the Blue Peter studio to show us all his equipment before the team set off for the Himalayas, we gave him something to take with him.

It was a flag which we hoped would be pinned to the shaft of an ice axe and flown from the highest point on earth—the summit of Mount Everest.

Chris is an old friend of Blue Peter. He had taken Peter to the top of Black Crag in the Lake District, and every terrifying moment was filmed by Mick Burke, a cameraman who had worked on dozens of Blue Peter stories. Now Chris, with Mick Burke, Dougal Haston, Doug Scott and twelve other climbers were about to make an attempt on the yet unscaled south-west face of the pinnacle of the world.

On the day of the Queen's coronation in 1953, Sir Edmund Hillary achieved ''the crowning glory'' as one newspaper headlined it, by becoming the first man ever to reach the summit of Everest. Several people have followed him, including a Japanese ladies' team. When Sir Edmund came to Blue Peter, he spoke with modesty and humour about ''the tourist route I took up Everest some years ago,'' although no one can take away his achievement of being the first man ever to stand on the roof of the world. But the south-west face has beaten them all. The 2000 metres of sheer rock rears up at the end of a five-week gruelling climb when altitude sickness, unbelievable cold, and sheer exhaustion begin to take their toll on the toughest of climbers.

Chris and Mick kept Blue Peter in touch with the expedition by sending back a series of specially filmed reports from the important stages of the climb. And we'd seen the Blue Peter flag flying from a little orange tent clinging to the side of the mountain. Then at 6.00 p.m. on 24 September, as the sun set on the roof of the world, Doug Scott and Dougal Haston became the first men to have got there by way of the treacherous south-west face.

Two days later, minutes after we on Blue Peter had been celebrating this magnificent achievement, news was flashed to John Craven's Newsround of a tragedy at the summit of Everest.

Mick Burke had set out with Martin Boysen to make another assault on the summit. Mick was carrying his camera and a Blue Peter flag. He had hoped to be the first man in the world to take moving pictures from the summit of Everest. His partner, Martin, had to turn back because one of his crampons had fallen off.

Mick carried on alone.

No one ever saw him again.

The weather, as it can in that unparalleled part of the world, had suddenly changed. A blizzard had blown up and Mick was gone for ever.

The expedition was abandoned, but Chris sent back a last report before leaving the mountain. He nailed a Blue Peter flag to his ice axe and planted it in a little pile of stones on the slopes of Everest.

''In memory,'' he said, ''of Mick Burke—a brave man and a good friend.''

READY

FOR ACTION

All expeditions need good equipment. With a strong tent and a warm sleeping-bag and a good night's sleep behind him, an explorer can face almost anything. Convert a couple of coat-hangers and some scrap material into a neat foldaway tent and your soldier doll will be all set to tackle the highest mountains or the Arctic wastes. Here's how to do it.

The Tent Frame

With some pliers, cut the hooks off two wire coat-hangers. They are made of pretty tough wire, so you might need someone with a strong wrist to give you a hand!

cut off hook

bend for feet

1

With the pliers, straighten out each hanger and turn the end of each ''leg'' outwards to make little feet. Fasten the two hangers together with sticky tape—and that's the frame completed. Just for the moment, tie a piece of cotton or fuse wire across the ends of the tent to stop it folding up while you fit the cover.

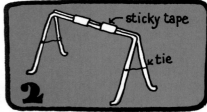

sticky tape

tie

2

The cover

Lay some scrap material over the frame and cut it neatly to fit. Don't stick or sew anything yet. You need to cut two triangles to fill the end in first. The easiest way is to stand the frame on end and then cut round it leaving about a centimetre extra all round.

The cover (continued)

Stand the frame up and lay the main cover back on top. Then dab glue all round the edges of the triangles and stick them to the cloth cover. Don't worry if it looks a bit rough. Wait till the glue dries, then turn the cover inside out and you'll find you've got a neat finish.

For the tent opening, cut up from the base of one end almost to the top of the tent. If you've got an old zip-fastener, you can glue this in to make the doorway. If not, make three holes in each side of the cut and thread string through to close the tent flap. When you've finished the "doorway", slide the cover on to the frame and fix it with a few stitches along the top bar. It won't matter if you don't, but it will stop it getting lost when you fold the tent up, between expeditions.

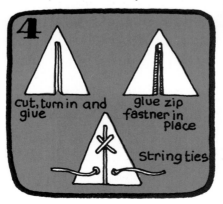

The Sleeping Bag

I used a piece of material from an old anorak, but anything will do. To get the size right, lay the explorer on the material and wrap it round him. When you cut it, leave plenty of material for the hems and remember not to make it too tight!

Fold the cut material inside out and glue all along the bottom and the side. Turn the top over about a couple of centimetres and glue that down, too. When the glue's dry, turn the bag inside out and the job's done. You'll have a tent and a sleeping-bag that will see your explorer safely through countless expeditions.

The case of the VANISHING VIOLIN

Can you solve this case?
Five careless mistakes give away
the crook. We spotted them—
can you?

As the last notes of the Mendelssohn Violin Concerto died away, the audience rose to its feet to give a tremendous ovation to Baxtrovich, the world-famous violinist. His performance had been perfect and the sound of his priceless Stradivarius violin had entranced everyone in the packed school hall.

Bob McCann heaved a sigh of relief. As leader of his school orchestra, he'd been worried all through the weeks of rehearsal in case something should go wrong. Not only did they have the honour of accompanying Baxtrovich as the school's guest artiste, but somewhere out in the audience was sitting Dr Johann Strumpfe, the great American impresario. If he'd been pleased with the orchestra's performance, Bob and his fellow musicians stood a good chance of representing British School Orchestras on a coast-to-coast summer tour of the United States.

"Well done, young man," said Baxtrovich, shaking Bob's hand as they walked off the platform. "Your orchestra is outstanding. Perhaps next time we meet it will be in America!"

"Sooner than that, sir," replied Bob. "I hope you will be at our reception later on this evening."

"It will be an honour and a pleasure," smiled the great man. "But listen, our public are demanding our presence once again." The applause rose to a crescendo as they walked back on to the stage.

Bob's uncle, Detective Inspector McCann, was in the audience. Leaning across to the small dark bearded man in front of him, he whispered:

"Do you think they'll make it to the States, Dr Strumpfe?"

"Too soon to say, but it was certainly a magnificent performance," he shouted over the applause.

"Perhaps then you'll be making an announcement at the reception?" queried the Inspector.

"Very probably. I will come a little late, because I have some business to attend to first, but I will be there

—never fear!"

Two hours later, Bob and the orchestra were entertaining their guests. Though no announcement had yet been made, a beaming Dr Strumpfe was half-way through his fifth sandwich. Baxtrovich, though, had not yet appeared! Bob was beginning to get worried.

"I hope he turns up before all the food runs out!" Bob said to his uncle.

"Don't worry, lad," laughed the Inspector. "I'll go and chat up Dr Strumpfe and maybe that will slow down his rate of consumption!"

Crossing over to the impresario, Inspector McCann asked him: "When will you announce your decision, Doctor? The boys are on tenterhooks!"

"As soon as Baxtrovich arrives. I can't think what is keeping him."

"Can you give me a hint, meanwhile?" asked McCann.

"I can only say that when I was a boy in New York and played in the Bronx Boys Orchestra, we would have been proud to have played even half so well as your boys have done tonight."

"Are you a New Yorker?" queried McCann.

"Yes. I was born beneath the shadow of the White House. And when I was a poor boy, I never thought that one day I would be invited there by President Ford himself to put on a concert."

"When was that?" asked McCann.

"Oh, in the spring of 1976. It was a special concert in celebration of the Three Hundred years of American Independence."

"It must have been a tremendous occasion. What did you play for the President?"

"His favourite, of course—and mine! Beethoven's 10th Symphony. And you know, my friend," he said, warming to the Inspector, "I have a marvellous recording of that symphony. It's on scratched old 78s, but it's conducted by the Maestro himself, Ludwig Van Beethoven!"

"Well I never," said the Inspector. "There can't be

many of those around!"

"No," said Dr Strumpfe, with a smile of satisfaction. "I picked it up in a little shop in a side street off the main road when I was motoring through Venice."

At that moment, the door burst open and a distraught Baxtrovich rushed in.

"My Stradivarius! My beautiful violin! It's gone!"

"Gosh" cried Bob. "It must be worth a fortune! What shall we do?"

"Nobody leave the room," shouted Dr Strumpfe, suddenly taking command. "What a terrible disgrace to your school," he said, looking at Bob with disgust. "Thank goodness I had not made any announcement. Boys like you are not fit to represent your country!"

"But—but," spluttered Bob, his face crumpled in distress.

"That's a bit strong, sir, isn't it?" snapped McCann. "Perhaps we should go back to your hotel and discuss this matter calmly."

"No. That will not be possible. I am leaving immediately," said the little man, trying to push past the dejected violinist.

"I think you'll find it will be possible," rasped McCann, grabbing the furious impresario by the arm. "Two of my men are there already, and so, unless I'm very much mistaken, are the lost Stradivarius and the real Dr Strumpfe!"

"What do you mean, Inspector?" cried Baxtrovich. "You have already recovered my violin?"

"I have indeed, sir!" he said, snapping the handcuffs on the struggling impostor. "The yard's been watching this man for some time and today he's made five very foolish mistakes! He's just a phoney impresario on the fiddle!"

Did you spot the five clues? Check your answers on page 76.

Bengo

by Tim

THE GUARDIAN
The Daily Telegraph

London's biggest evening sale
Evening News

DAILY EXPRESS

Evening Standard

Daily Mirror · **THE Sun**

Daily Mail

WEDNESDAY, MARCH 16, 1976   6p

Jason, the cat star of TV's 'Blue Peter' dies

By RICHARD LAST, Television Staff

...st-known cat, Jason, who made 952 ... on the B B C television children's ... ue Peter," has died in his 12th year. ... television "star" since he was three

Jason, a sealpoint Siamese, made his TV debut in June, 1964. His last appearance was on Thursday, only a few hours before he died of kidney failure at his home ... Sussex early yeste...

During...

simply...

A sp... ...m for the programme said: "He was a substitute pet for all the children who could not have one of their own.

Jason

Daily Mail, Saturday, January 17, 1976

Jason with 'Blue Peter' girl Lesley Judd

... **million fans**

have shared him with us. 'Fortunately his deat... quick and he suffered ...always amazed viewer...

Jason, TV's coolest cat, dies

By James M...

Jason ... kids' TV favourite

Top cat Jason dies after 952 TV shows

JASON, the TV cat loved by millions of young viewers, has

Jason the TV cat star dies

MIRROR

Famous British Cat Dies At 11

LONDON (UPI) — Jason, a Siamese cat, joined the children's program "Blue Peter" on British television 11 years ago when he was three weeks old. A generation of children grew up with him.

Jason died Friday, just after making his 952nd telev...

...Britain's...

"The e... painless," said program editor Biddy Baxter. She said Jason died of kidney failure.

Jan 20, 1976
The Post-Journal

GOODBYE JASON

Life and death of a TV star

By CLIFFORD DAVIS, M...

MOST POPULAR U.K. CAT DIES

These were the very sad headlines in newspapers all over the world on Saturday, 17 January 1976.

If you think it's strange for the death of a British cat to hit the headlines in newspapers like the *Ceylon Daily News*, the *Vancouver Province* and the *Post-Journal* in New York, as well as Britain's national papers and on the TV and radio news, you have to remember Jason was no ordinary moggie. No other cat has been a TV programme star, seen by millions of viewers each week, for over eleven years. And no other cat has ever had such an enormous postbag. For his eleventh birthday, Jason received over one thousand cards, which certainly goes to prove how tremendously popular he was.

Like Petra, his name was chosen by "Blue Peter" viewers, and all his training and upbringing were shown on the programme.

Jason's first appearance on Television was when he was three weeks old. He came to the studio with his mother, Victoria, and his brother and sister. Since then, he'd taken part in 952 programmes and had travelled hundreds of miles all over Britain to take part in cat shows and to be guest of honour on all kinds of important occasions. Working in the Blue Peter studio must have been good training, because he was always very well behaved and was never ruffled by crowds of people or strange animals.

Jason hadn't lost many of his nine lives. His worst accident was when he was attacked by a wild Tom Cat when he was a kitten. He was knocked over so violently, his back leg was broken, but he had the fracture pinned, and was a model patient, and the leg soon healed. Another time, Jason was ill after playing with a frog. But we washed his mouth out with milk of magnesia and gave him some medicine to get rid of the poison, and he was none the worse for his adventure.

Jason sired two lots of kittens, Burmese/Siamese hybrids and pure Seal Pointed Siamese like himself. He became a father for the first time in May 1965, and a grandfather in 1966.

Rather like Petra and Shep, Jason was always conscious that the Blue Peter studio was *his* territory, and he could be quite fierce when any other cats took part in the programme. On the other hand, he was always good with dogs and tolerated five bouncy puppies during his life—our three guide dog pups as well as Patch and Shep.

Jason was always very popular with visiting celebrities. He'd been stroked by Princess Anne, Ringo Starr, David Cassidy and Dame Margot Fonteyn to name but a few. But perhaps the celebrity he enjoyed meeting the most of all was the world-famous violinist, Yehudi Menuhin—and he sat entranced as he listened to the music.

It's always very sad when a much-loved pet dies. But we know Jason had a happy life, and fortunately, when he died of kidney failure he suffered no pain. To us there'll never be another cat quite like Jason!

CANAL JUMPING

It's hard to believe that Canal Jumping is not only a sport, but a national one at that. And if I hadn't watched a champion in action, I might not have taken it at all seriously.

But as soon as the football season stops, the people of Friesland in the North Eastern corner of Holland get out their 11 metre long wooden poles and make for the nearest canal, and all the strenuous and usually very wet practice ends in the Annual Championships that take place every summer.

Canal Jumping, or Fierljeppen to give it its proper name, may look like a game from *It's a Knockout*, but it's taken very seriously by the Frieslanders. It's a sort of pole vaulting over water, and the record stands at around 17 metres.

There's a run up of about 30 metres that ends in a ramp. As you near the canal bank, you have to make a well-timed grab for your pole—held by an official—and then hurl yourself across the cold, muddy water, rather like a monkey on a stick. If your speed and balance are right, you glide over in a semicircle and reach the other bank in safety. If you're too slow, you fall slap bang in the middle of the canal, which is what I did six times!

The crowds thought it was a great laugh—especially when a girl champion about half my size sailed effortlessly in front of me, right across the canal—without even wetting her big toe.

But after my first ignominious soaking, I realised what some of the laughs were about. I was wearing brand-new swimming trunks for the first time, and when I clambered on to the bank and looked down, I saw to my horror they were absolutely transparent! I reckon my face went as red as a piece of Dutch cheese. It was all very embarrassing, until our film cameraman took pity on me and gave me the clapper board to hold in front of me. In the end, someone lent me another pair of trunks and we had to start our filming all over again. You can be quite sure I won't forget my day's Fierljeppen in a hurry!

MONSTER MYSTERIES

Thanks to the latest archaeological and electronic detective work, new light has been thrown on two of Britain's largest monsters.

We spread the bones of one of them out in the Blue Peter studio—an amphibious reptile between 130 and 150 million years old. They were discovered in April 1975 in what's proving to be a Monster burial ground in the most extraordinary place—it's under the foundry of the British Rail works at Swindon!

The bones belonged to a 9-metre-long short-necked Plesiosaur and it's the third monster to have been dug up at Swindon.

The first, in 1921, was discovered by workmen digging a hole for a large steel pillar. They had quite a shock when they found the fossilised bones of what was said to be an Ichthyosaurus, about 6 metres below the surface.

Although experts were called, weeks went by and no one turned up. So incredibly, the pillar was simply put in position and the hole filled with concrete—leaving the bones where they were!

Twenty-nine years later, workmen digging half a mile away found three bits of fossilised vertebrae of *another* Ichthyosaurus, and an eyewitness on both those occasions was Mr William Gardner who has just retired after 50 years in Railway Engineering. When the third lot of bones was found only a short distance from the Ichthyosaurus vertebrae, we met Mr Gardner who showed us where the previous discoveries were made, and there can't be many people who've been connected with three such exciting

palaentological discoveries quite by chance!

The most recent find is probably the most outstanding. This time there was immediate identification by an expert—Dr Beverley Halstead of Reading University. When Dr Halstead brought the bones to the studio, he explained that the short-necked Plesiosaur is very rare indeed. It's

Mr William Gardner who eye-witnessed three exciting excavations at British Rail's Swindon foundry.

Hemel Hempstead Fire Brigade built this monster model in an attempt to lure Nessie to the surface of Loch Ness.

much less common than the long-necked kind that we helped to dig up at Peterborough five years ago, and Dr Halstead believes the Swindon discovery may be the world's best.

The bones are now in safe keeping at the British Museum, and who knows how many more dinosaurs are waiting to be dug up under what's just about one of the most important railway engineering centres in the world.

Scotland's Loch Ness monster is also thought by some monster hunters to be a plesiosaur. The Hemel Hempstead Fire Brigade's huge model was floated on the Loch in an attempt to lure Nessie to the surface, but like dozens of other attempts, it failed. Over the years, quite a few photographs alleged to be Nessie have been proved to have been fakes. In December 1975 a man admitted that pictures he'd said he'd taken *forty-one* years previously had been a hoax!

But in spite of the jokes and publicity stunts, there are scientists who've spent years studying all the reported sightings. We joined the American team that was taking under-water film at Loch Ness. They found a sonar trace had appeared on their equipment, proving something large had passed by their cameras.

When the film was developed, there was world-wide interest in a photograph showing what was supposed to be the fin of a monster 3 metres long and one metre wide. On the strength of this and other underwater photographs, a group of scientists, including Sir Peter Scott, gave Nessie its first scientific name—Nessiteras Rhombopteryx—which means "a diamond-shaped Loch Ness monster with diamond-shaped fins". Some people have pointed out that it's also an anagram of "Monster Hoax by Sir Peter S!"

Blue Peter viewers have taken Nessie photographs, too—like those by 7-year-old Ian Wilkins and his father Alan which showed a black dot moving in the water.

Yet more evidence turned up in January 1976 when a British electronics company claimed to have measured a huge, unexplained body in Loch Ness with "electro-videosonic" high frequency sound waves. Their instruments recorded an object at least $7\frac{1}{2}$ metres long, 150 metres down, and the team hopes that Nessie will be brought to the surface and then trapped in a section of the Caledonian Canal. The idea is that when the canal is drained, the monster will be revealed. That could cause problems, though, because under the existing regulations, the capture of a Loch Ness monster would end in a fine of £100. On the other hand, the offer made by a daily newspaper fourteen years ago still stands—a reward of £10,000 for conclusive proof of the monster's existence.

But so far, Nessie remains Britain's biggest Monster Mystery!

Take it easy with

HARD TIMES BISCUITS AND FRUITADE

Times may be hard—but even if you're down to your last few pence, you can live like a lord with my Hard Times biscuits and cheap Fruitade.

These are two recipes that are really economical. At the same time they taste delicious and would be very useful for a party or picnic.

You can make about twenty biscuits from this recipe. The fruitade recipe makes approximately a litre of concentrated juice. The citric acid acts as a preservative so the juice can be kept for up to three weeks (refrigerated). This recipe is a particularly cheap one and works out at less than 1p per glass when diluted with water.

BISCUITS

Ingredients:
5 oz. (125 g) fat
2 oz. (50 g) sugar (brown or white)
2½ oz. (65 g) porridge oats and
2½ oz. (65 g) self-raising flour
   mixed together
1 egg
Glacé cherries (optional)

FRUITADE

Ingredients:
1 orange   1 lemon
(You could also use grapefruit—or a mixture of all three)
½ oz. (15 g) citric acid
1 lb. (500 g) sugar
1 pint (500 ml) water

Method

1 Put fat (half margarine and half lard) into a mixing bowl, and cream until smooth.

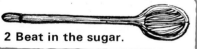

2 Beat in the sugar.

3 Add the egg (or two left-over yolks or whites).
4 Add the mixed oats and flour.

5 When all the ingredients have been beaten together roll the mixture into balls about the size of a walnut, then place on a *greased* baking tray.

6 Slightly flatten the tops of the biscuits, then if you like you can place half a glacé cherry on the top of each. (N.B. Remember to allow enough space between the biscuits for the mixture to spread when it's cooking).

7 Put the trays in the oven at Regulo 325°F (Gas Mark 3) and let the biscuits cook for about 10 to 15 minutes.

8 After removing the trays from the oven, lift the biscuits from the tray with a spatula, place on a wire tray to cool.

9 When cool, the biscuits are ready to eat. Store any left over in an airtight tin.

Method

1 Grate the rind off the orange and the lemon and put the rind into a mixing bowl.

2 Squeeze the orange and lemon and add the juice to the rinds.
3 Add the citric acid and the sugar and stir well.

4 Boil the water in a kettle. The water must be boiling, so ask a grown-up to help you with this.
5 Carefully pour the boiling water on to the mixture then set aside to cool.

6 When cold, strain through a sieve to get rid of all the bits of rind.
7 Then bottle, and the fruitade is ready to serve, diluted with water.

63

PUZZLES

WHICH ONE WILL GET TO THE MILK?

MEMORY TEST

LOOK AT THE OBJECTS BELOW FOR TWO MINUTES. CLOSE THE BOOK AND SEE HOW MANY OF THE OBJECTS YOU CAN REMEMBER.

WHAT'S WRONG WITH THIS PICTURE? THERE ARE 8 MISTAKES TO FIND

TEST OF STRENGTH

SHOW YOUR FRIENDS JUST HOW STRONG YOU ARE. PLACE THE PALM OF YOUR HAND ON TOP OF YOUR HEAD. BY HOLDING YOUR ARM AS SHOWN ABOVE SEE IF YOUR FRIEND CAN RAISE YOUR HAND FROM YOUR HEAD. IT'S QUITE AMAZING!

BLUE PETER SPECIAL ASSIGNMENT

Have you ever been to a place where a famous person has lived long ago and felt their presence so strongly you could almost see them—sitting in their favourite chair—walking down a corridor—or strolling through the garden?

In this year's Blue Peter Special Assignment we've tried to create that strange feeling.

Actors dressed and made up to look exactly like six famous personalities have visited the houses they lived in, and we've been able to go back in time and bring to life some of the great moments in history.

1. Lesley, who began her career as a dancer, visits the home of Anna Pavlova, the famous ballerina.
2. "The house is ugly. It looks neither old nor new, but it has a capital study," said Charles Darwin who made one of the world's greatest discoveries at Down House.
3. John Keats fell in love with the girl next door and wrote some of the world's greatest poetry at Wentworth Place.
4. Sir Walter Raleigh brought tobacco to England and a servant drenched him when he was smoking in his home at Sherborne Castle.
5. "I consider the whole of this work to be perfect," declared the Prince Regent as he surveyed his new summer Palace, the Royal Marine Pavilion at Brighton.
6. "Everyone loves flattery and when it comes to Royalty you should lay it on with a trowel," said Benjamin Disraeli, Queen Victoria's favourite Prime Minister.

For 200 years Brighton has been a favourite holiday place where everyone goes to have a good time enjoying the sun and the sea. In the heart of Brighton is a strange building of domes and towers, something out of the Arabian Nights. It is called the Royal Pavilion, for once Brighton was the seaside home of a British Prince.

Prince Regent
AT BRIGHTON

George, Prince of Wales, son of King George III, was young, good-looking, and a leader of Society — a real Prince Charming. Prinny, as the country called him, made Brighton fashionable.

It was a little village called Brighthelmstone when 21-year-old George first visited it. A famous doctor had said the place was very healthy, so people were beginning to build houses there. When George saw the fishing village, the shingle beach and the white cliffs, he fell in love with it straight away.

He also fell in love with Maria Fitzherbert — she was attractive and clever, but of course she was not royal. She was a Roman Catholic, too, and the Prince knew he would never gain the King's consent to his marriage. Mrs Fitzherbert lived at Richmond, and a song was written about her —

"I'd crowns resign,
To call thee mine —
Sweet lass of Richmond Hill."

The Prince made up his mind to marry her, even without the King's permission, and a secret wedding was performed. Then he took his beloved bride to his beloved Brighton, and for a while they were very happy.

"Dearest of wives — I will remain until the latest moments of my existence, unalterably thine," the Prince declared as they exchanged lockets.

They settled down in a little house by the sea, but soon the Prince wanted something bigger and more suitable. He consulted architects and told them he did not want an ordinary, stuffy royal palace, but a light, sunny, attractive home by the sea, so the idea of the Royal Pavilion was born. Over the years, the Prince changed it, enlarged it, redecorated it, so the present pavilion was not his first idea — but is really as the Prince eventually planned it.

The outside, with its domes and gold arches, is Indian. But the inside is all Chinese, with dragons, and mandarins, and Chinese ladies, so that it is like being in the middle of a Chinese lantern.

Other people hated it, or laughed at it, but the Prince loved it.

"I consider the whole of this work as perfect," he proclaimed.

But it cost a terrible amount of money, and soon his debts amounted to a million pounds. He asked the King and Parliament to help, but they would do so on one condition — he must part from Maria Fitzherbert and marry a princess, to provide the country with an heir to the throne. At first the Prince indignantly refused, but in the end, his debts were so pressing he had to give way. Mrs Fitzherbert quietly left the country.

The bride chosen for George was a German princess, his cousin Caroline of Brunswick. She was coarse, loud-voiced and dirty, and George, the First Gentleman of Europe, disliked her on sight. She said he was too fat and ugly. The new royal couple hated each other from the start. "I had rather see toads and vipers crawling over my victuals than sit at the same table with her."

But there was one good result of the marriage — an heir to the throne was born — a daughter, Princess Charlotte. She was the darling of the whole country, and everyone sympathised with her mother and blamed the Prince for their separation. Whenever he appeared in public, people shouted "Where's your wife, Georgie?"

He was still the leader of fashion, and the smart set flocked to Brighton, where he spent much of his time, and they all longed to receive an invitation to the Royal Pavilion.

The Prince was a delightful host, and he gave dinner parties for about 24 people. The table sparkled with

George, Prince of Wales, secretly married Maria Fitzherbert and took her to his beloved Brighton.

They lived happily by the sea, but soon the Prince wanted a proper royal residence.

He designed the Royal Pavilion. "I consider the whole of this work as perfect," he said.

It cost so much he owed vast sums of money. The King and Parliament made him part from Maria Fitzherbert.

The Prince was forced to marry Caroline of Brunswick, but he hated her.

"I would rather see toads and vipers crawling over my victuals than sit at the same table with her."

The Prince gave luxurious dinner parties in his Pavilion at Brighton.

Hundreds of cooks worked in the kitchens preparing the huge meals the Prince loved.

glass, silver and porcelain; the whole room was ablaze with lights; Chinese dragons ran riot everywhere, and enchanting panels in a Chinese style decorated the walls. From the centre of the domed ceiling hung the most fantastic object in the whole of the fantastic Pavilion—an enormous hanging lamp, like flying dragons, and lit by science's latest discovery—gas. It had cost five thousand, six hundred and thirteen pounds, nine shillings, and weighed almost a ton.

Behind the scenes, a few yards away, a well-planned kitchen was a hive of industry. "Such contrivances for roasting, boiling, baking, stewing, frying, steaming and heating" one visitor described admiringly. The kitchen needed to be good—one menu, served on 15 January 1817, lists 116 dishes! If the Prince ate in that style every night of his life, no wonder he grew so stout in middle age!

By now the old King George III was ill and incapable of ruling the country. Prinny became the Prince Regent, though he did not have a king's powers, and the Crown seemed as far out of his grasp as ever. Princess Caroline still pestered him, and scandalous tales were told of her.

Their daughter, Princess Charlotte, grew up, and made a happy marriage. She was to have a child— but very sadly, the baby died, and Princess Charlotte herself died a few days afterwards.

It was a horrible moment for her father—he had lost his daughter, the heir to the throne, and the whole wretched business of his marriage and the separation from Maria Fitzherbert had been utterly useless.

Then—at long last—George III died, aged 81. The Prince Regent was proclaimed King George IV—he was nearly sixty years old. He made up his mind that he would never allow Caroline to appear at his side as his Queen. On Coronation Day, Caroline made a great scene at the door of Westminster Abbey, but she was not allowed in. She went away and died soon after.

The new king tried to rule as a sensible monarch. He had a new suite of rooms designed at the Pavilion, in black and gold, which were very splendid, but rather sad. They looked like an old man's rooms, turning their back on light and life, a complete contrast to the rest of the sunny Pavilion.

George became ill, and knew the end was near. He asked that he should be buried wearing all the

The Prince's daughter might have been Queen, but she died young.

adornments he should be wearing at the time of his death—and afterwards his attendants understood why.

Round his neck, on a black ribbon, he wore a picture of Maria Fitzherbert. When she was told about this, Mrs Fitzherbert, who had married the King nearly fifty years before, said nothing—but large tears fell down her cheeks.

After his death, the newspapers made savage attacks on him; for many years the Pavilion was abandoned and derelict.

Then in the last quarter of a century, it has come to life again. Decorations have been replaced, the golden dragons have been restored, even the furniture has been discovered and put back.

Today the Pavilion looks as it did in the Prince Regent's day, when honoured guests gathered after a luxurious banquet and the First Gentleman of Europe himself sang for their entertainment in his own Pavilion —a Royal Palace and a work of love.

Footnote: 10 weeks after we finished filming at the Pavilion came reports of a disastrous fire. Part of the beautiful Music Room was destroyed and experts say it will cost at least £180,000 of today's money to restore this Pavilion to the Palace the Prince Regent once loved.

An enormous gas light blazed over the dinner table.

The Prince Regent was nearly sixty years old before he became King George IV.

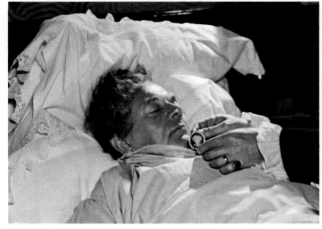

When he died, George IV was wearing round his neck a picture of Maria Fitzherbert.

Today the Prince's Marine Pavilion is the pride of Brighton.

CHRISTMAS STAR

A bright star was the first sign of the very first Christmas. Why not welcome every Christmas with a shiny star you've made yourself? It won't take long, and it's cheap, too! We've made ours from a sheet of gold wrapping paper, but any kind will do. Painted or coloured, any way you like and finished off with any trimmings left over from your Christmas tree or parcels, a star like this makes a superb decoration you can use over and over again.

Even if you can't draw a star, you'll be able to make this one. Just see how easy it is!

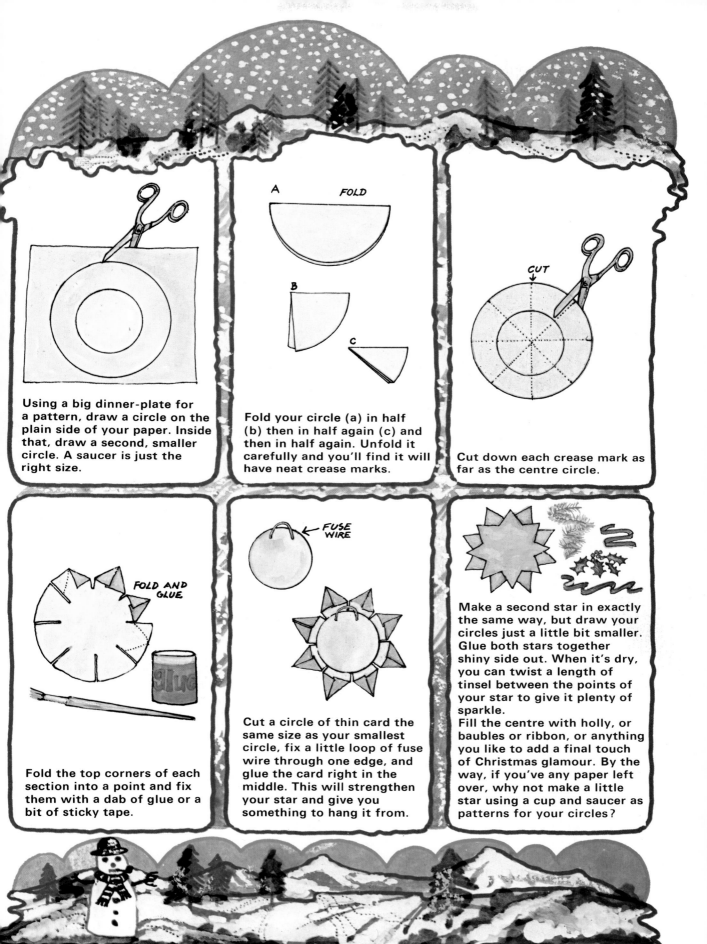

Using a big dinner-plate for a pattern, draw a circle on the plain side of your paper. Inside that, draw a second, smaller circle. A saucer is just the right size.

Fold your circle (a) in half (b) then in half again (c) and then in half again. Unfold it carefully and you'll find it will have neat crease marks.

Cut down each crease mark as far as the centre circle.

Fold the top corners of each section into a point and fix them with a dab of glue or a bit of sticky tape.

Cut a circle of thin card the same size as your smallest circle, fix a little loop of fuse wire through one edge, and glue the card right in the middle. This will strengthen your star and give you something to hang it from.

Make a second star in exactly the same way, but draw your circles just a little bit smaller. Glue both stars together shiny side out. When it's dry, you can twist a length of tinsel between the points of your star to give it plenty of sparkle.
Fill the centre with holly, or baubles or ribbon, or anything you like to add a final touch of Christmas glamour. By the way, if you've any paper left over, why not make a little star using a cup and saucer as patterns for your circles?

THREE GIRLS ON A ROCK

"Let's send Lesley," they said. "After all, it's International Women's year." Every Friday afternoon in a small room in the East Tower, our fates are decided by the Editor and the two producers of "Blue Peter." On that particular Friday afternoon, they nearly settled my fate for good, although nobody realised it at the time.

The film they were planning was a visit to the Bishop Rock lighthouse which stands above the sea six miles off the most westerly part of Britain. The only way to get there is by being winched off a boat by rope and swung across the waves as they crash over the Bishop Rock.

Three weeks after that meeting, on 18 May 1975 (a day that's engraved on my memory for ever), I was in Mike Hicks' little boat, heaving up and down the swell, and staring up at the towering lighthouse. The director, Sarah Hellings, her assistant Denise, and I, huddled in the bows of the boat and looked at the pounding waves and jagged rocks as we surged backwards and forwards.

"I don't really fancy this, Sarah," I said.

Sarah, Denise and I got our first sight of the Bishop Rock lighthouse.

A tiny figure on the Rock flung out a rope that was to carry us to the lighthouse.

Sarah looked every bit as anxious as I felt.

"Neither do I," she said. "But I don't much fancy going back and telling them we've failed, either."

Mike slipped a canvas belt over my head and pulled it tight under my arms. The belt was tied to a length of rope which went straight to a winch at the top of the lighthouse and down into the hands of two men standing at the base.

"Hang on tight with your hands, Lesley," he shouted over the surf. "When they pull, it'll come with a jerk."

It came with a jerk, all right. Seconds after I left the deck, my canvas belt slipped straight down my body and was left dangling uselessly beneath my feet. I was hanging on with nothing but my hands! I shot up high in the air, not daring to look down into the sea. My arms were being wrenched from their sockets and my hands were burning on the rope. I really was sick with terror. And all the time I kept thinking—"If by a miracle I get there, I've still got to come back!"

I landed into the reassuring arms of Larry Walker, a large man with *Bishop Rock* written convincingly across the front of his sweater. Then one of those strange, ludicrous things happened which seem reserved for the most solemn or terrifying moments in your life. I was looking in an incredulous way at the skinless fingers that had miraculously been able to stay clenched round that rope when Larry very formally took hold of my hand, shook it and said, "Welcome to Bishop Rock! It's very nice to see you, Lesley."

Sarah and Denise made the same heart-stopping journey and exactly the same thing happened to them! The Bishop Rock breeches buoy just didn't seem to be designed for ladies!

When I landed on the narrow ledge round the base of the lighthouse, I thought I was there. But I wasn't quite; there was one more treat in store. A metal rung ladder ran 12 metres vertically up the side of the lighthouse to the front door. I went up first, followed by Sarah, Denise, and the camera crew. When we all got to the top, Sarah turned to the cameraman and said.

"Oh blast it. I'd intended to take a shot of Lesley climbing up that ladder." They all turned and looked at me.

"All right," I said, climbing down the ladder ready to make the

"I don't really fancy this," I said to Sarah. "Neither do I, but I don't much fancy going back and telling them we've failed," she replied.

Seconds after this picture was taken the belt slipped straight down my body and I was left hanging on with nothing but my hands!

Once aboard, I climbed up inside the light to reach lighthouse keeper Andy Bluer.

"Welcome aboard Bishop Rock, love," said Andy, who was polishing the glass with a yellow duster.

ascent again. "I don't think I can get *more* frightened anyway!"

I had been warned that lighthouse keepers are generally strong, silent men who don't have much to say for themselves. After all, if you live on one of the world's loneliest places, no one would expect you to be a chatterer!

But that certainly wasn't true of Andy Bluer who was one of the kindest, most hospitable, funniest and *chattiest* men I've met since I joined Blue Peter. He was also wearing a *Bishop Rock* jersey, but with a huge white beard, and very twinkly blue eyes. I expected him to be a west countryman, but Andy comes from up North in Lancashire. He took me up inside the light which is one of the most eerie experiences I've ever had. Standing in the middle of space, surrounded by prisms and lenses revolving and changing colour as the sun caught them, and then revealing glimpses of a weird, distorted sea, it was like a cross between outer space and Top of the Pops. I enjoyed talking to Andy, but I must admit that the thought of the journey back to the boat never quite left my mind. He took me out on the balcony with commanding views of the sea and showed me the dreaded winch that had pulled us aboard.

"Don't worry, love, it's designed to carry half a ton, so I think you'll be all right!"

I looked out across the sea again, trying to take my mind off the winch.

"There's no sign of Mike's boat yet," I said.

He took me up to the topmost balcony and showed me the winch that had pulled me aboard.

High inside the light, surrounded by glass prisms, it was like standing in the middle of space.

The journey back to the boat was even more terrifying than the journey out.

"That's because you're looking towards America, love," he grinned. "It usually takes about three weeks that way. The boat will be round the other side."

"Let's make sure you're well in this time," said Larry, giving the harness an extra tug round my chest.

"I just want to check something," I said. Anything to delay that sickening moment!

The belt held this time, but the sensation of dropping *down* towards that surging sea was infinitely worse. My stomach seemed to come up into my mouth, and at one point, I could actually feel spray from the waves on my back. When I looked up and saw the boat *above* me, with Mike and his mate struggling to pull me in, I really thought I was done for. I remember calling out weakly—

"Grab me—Grab me!" which looking back on it seemed a rather unnecessary thing to say.

Sarah, Denise and the crew followed. The last man was stills photographer, John Jefford, who came down wearing a helmet camera which supplied the really sick-making "eyeline" shots of the sea and the bobbing boat.

As we waved goodbye to Andy, Sarah turned to me and said, "Well, we've done it!"

"Yes, we have," I said. And I couldn't help feeling proud—of all three of us.

Denise, who at 1½ metres is even shorter than I am, looked up from the notebook she had even carried down the rope with her.

"Just one thing, Sarah," she said. "We're never going to do it again, are we?"

PUZZLE PICTURES

1 On 15 March 1976 our **Tree for the Year 2000** measured 4 metres 10 cm.
2 The **Forth Road Bridge**—Europe's longest.
3 Lesley's **Christmas measles**.
4 Outsize chess men from the **Bulldog Drummond** film.
5 Arriving at **Number 10 Downing Street** for the Prime Minister's Christmas Party for disabled children.
6 Protecting one of our cameras from **Rod Hull's Emu**.
7 This giant pink hippo belonged to Mr Michael Whiteway of Reading.
8 **Montreal Ted**—the British Olympic team's mascot.
9 These six-metre **blades of corn** were designed by artist Andrew Logan.
10 **Dianthus Button**—or Bertie Buttons for short— **Cruft's Supreme Champion** 1976.
11 Wrestling Olympic style with the **Abbots Langley Tigers**.
12 Stuck in **Lock 44** on the **Southern Stratford Canal**.

WHAT'S WRONG WITH PICTURE (page 64)

1 No bottom to bus stop sign
2 Moustache on lady
3 No top to the man's hat
4 No newspaper—although man appears to be holding one
5 No lapel on man's coat
6 Different trouser leg
7 Lady has only one leg
8 Man at the end has no shoes

THE CASE OF THE VANISHING VIOLIN

1 The impostor said he was born in New York beneath the shadow of the White House. The White House is not in New York. It is in Washington.
2 Dr Strumpfe said the concert was in celebration of 300 years of American Independence. If he had really arranged it, he would have known that 1976 is the *200th* anniversary.
3 He said the music was Beethoven's 10th Symphony. Beethoven only wrote 9 symphonies.
4 He said a record of Beethoven conducting. This is impossible. Beethoven died long before gramophone records were invented.
5 He could not have motored along the main road in Venice as there are no roads or cars—only canals and boats.

USEFUL INFORMATION

Turkish Tourism Information Office,
49 Conduit Street, London W.1.

Gladstone Pottery Museum,
Longton, Stoke-on-Trent. Tel. Stoke-on-Trent 319232 for times of opening.

Riding for The Disabled Association,
Avenue 'R', National Agricultural Centre, Kenilworth, Warks.

Mount Everest Foundation,
c/o The Royal Geographical Society, Kensington Gore, London S.W.7.

Natural History Museum,
Cromwell Road, London S.W.7.

Dutch National Tourist Board,
143 New Bond Street, London W.1.

BLUE PETER SPECIAL ASSIGNMENT FILMS

were made at the following houses. (Telephone to check opening times).

The Prince Regent
The Royal Pavilion, Brighton. Tel. Brighton 63005.

Darwin
Down House (Darwin Museum), Luxted Road, Down, Kent. Tel. Farnborough 53649 (day) 59119 (night).

Pavlova
Ivy House, North End Road, Golders Green, N.W.11. Tel. 01-435-8377.

Keats
Keats House, Wentworth Place, Keats Grove, N.W.3. Tel. 01-435-2062.

Disraeli
Hughenden Manor, High Wycombe, Bucks. Tel. High Wycombe 28051.

Raleigh
Sherborne Castle, Sherborne, Dorset. Tel. Sherborne 2072 and Tower of London. Tel. 01-709-0765.

GO WITH NOAKES!

Grasmere Sports takes place each year on the third Thursday in August. Details from Mr G. A. Ashton, Rydal Road, Ambleside.

The Milk Race lasts for two weeks and starts each year on Spring Bank Holiday Monday. Further information from The Milk Marketing Board, Thames Ditton, Surrey.

The Oxford Bumps lasts for four days and takes place in the fifth week of Oxford Trinity (Summer) term. For further information write to The Secretary, Oxford University Boat Club, Iffley Road, Oxford.

Formula 5000. Details of motor racing at Oulton Park from Mr R. Foster, Cheshire Car Circuit, Little Budworth, Tarporley, Cheshire.

Guernsey Handicap: The Royal Channel Islands Yacht Club organise a number of races during the summer. Details from The Secretary, Royal Channel Islands Yacht Club, Quay Steps, St Peter Port, Guernsey, C.I.

The Red Arrows: Details of displays from The Team Manager, The Red Arrows, RAF Kemble, Nr Cirencester, Glos.

ACKNOWLEDGEMENTS

PHOTOGRAPHS IN THIS BOOK were taken by: Joan Williams, Charles Walls, Barry Boxall, John Jefford, John Adcock, Michael Cook & Rosemary Gill, with the exception of picture 7 on page 5 by Topix; top right and bottom left (page 11) by permission of Grasmere Sports Committee; Canal Jumping photographs on page 58 by VVV Friesland; The Royal Pavilion (pages 66 & 69) from the Royal Pavilion, Brighton; View of Brighthelmstone (page 66) from Mary Evans Picture Library; George IV (page 66) Caroline of Brunswick (page 68) and George IV (page 69) from the National Portrait Gallery; Lesley's beetle (page 41) by R. D. Pope; Everest Summit photograph (page 48) by permission of British Everest Expedition 1975/Barclays Bank International; background picture (page 62) from Radio Times Hulton Picture Library; The monster illustration (page 46) was reproduced from *The Phantom Tollbooth* by Norman Juster, illustrated by Jules Feiffer, pub. Collins; *Lifeline* was written by Dorothy Smith; *The Eglinton Tournament* and illustrations on page 25 were by Robert Broomfield; *Bleep & Booster*, Bengo and the *Mystery Picture* by "Tim"; *Inside Story* by Geoffrey Wheeler.

BIDDY BAXTER, EDWARD BARNES AND ROSEMARY GILL WOULD LIKE TO ACKNOWLEDGE THE HELP OF GILLIAN FARNSWORTH AND MARGARET PARNELL.

DESIGNED BY EILEEN STRANGE AND JOHN STRANGE.

Blue Peter COMPETITION

Would you like to meet John, Peter, Lesley and the rest of the Blue Peter team? Would you like to see all the animals? Would you like to come to London and have tea with them all? This is your chance!

Just solve this puzzle. It's very easy—but watch out! There's more than one answer! If you can send us the solution that compares EXACTLY with John, Peter and Lesley's answers YOU could be invited to come to an exciting

BLUE PETER PARTY

There will be lots of competition badges for the runners-up, too!
When you have finished the puzzle, send it with the entry form to: Blue Peter Competition, BBC Television Centre, London W.12.

ACROSS
2. Girl's name
4. Boy's name
6. Prefix
9. Number

DOWN
1. Character in this book
3. Abbreviation for the morning
5. Fifth month of the year
7. Opposite of fat
8. Small child

First prize winners and runners-up will be notified by letter. The closing date for entries is **10 January 1977**.

	1 B		2 P			3 A
B	L	U	E			M
	E		4 T	O	5 M	
6 R	E		E		A	7 T
			P	A	8 R	T	Y	H
					O		I
9 F	O	U	R	T	E	E	N

NAME *Anne Rogerson*

ADDRESS *15, Munro Road.*
Glasgow G13 1SQ

AGE *10*

1ST TO THE TOP

A GAME FOR TWO TO FOUR PLAYERS. START AT BASE CAMP. THROW THE DICE IN TURN AND MOVE TO THE NUMBER SHOWN ON THE DICE. THE FIRST PLAYER TO REACH NO. 56 IS THE WINNER AND WILL HAVE CLIMBED THE MOUNTAIN FIRST. ITS A HARD CLIMB WITH LOTS OF DANGER SO—
GOOD LUCK!

42

43

DROP PACK GO TO COLLECT AT 25

41

40

BASE CAMP FOUR MISS ONE TURN

39

19

20

LOSE DIRECTION MISS ONE TURN

21 ENTER CAVE GO TO 38

22

18

17

16 FALL INTO CREVASSE MISS ONE TURN

BASE CAMP

1

2 CROSS SNOW BRIDGE TO 14